Paul
CÉZANNE

Paul CÉZANNE

PHILIPPE CROS

BARNES
&NOBLE

NEW YORK

© **EDIGROUP/EDITIONS TERRAIL, Paris 2006**

This 2006 edition published by Barnes & Noble, Inc.
by arrangement with Edigroup.

Editorial staff
Soline Massot and Anne Zweibaum
Layout
Duetto édition, Nelly Maurel
Iconography
Hélène Orizet
Copy editor
Christophe Gallier
Lithography
L'Exprimeur, Paris

ISBN 13: 978-0-7607-9006-9
ISBN 10: 0-7607-9006-X

Printed and bound in China

1 3 5 7 9 10 8 6 4 2

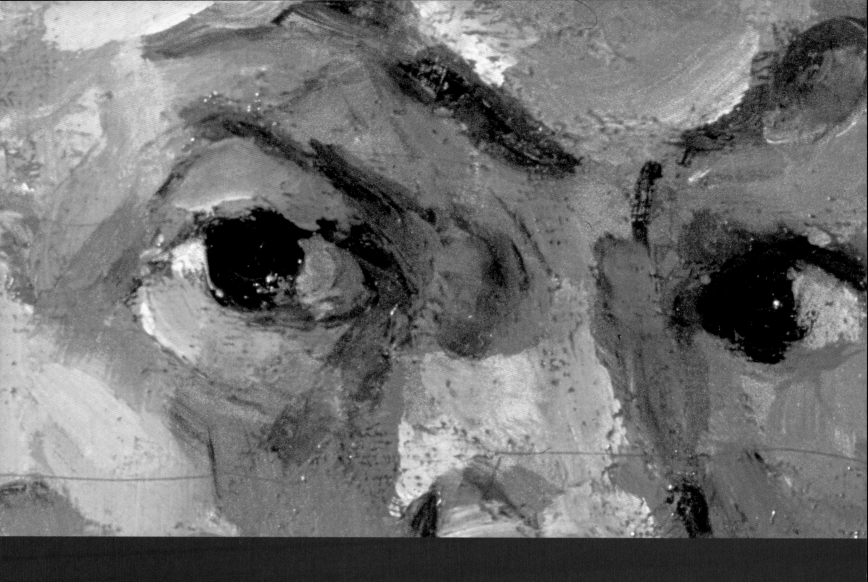

Summary

From Aix to Paris: from childhood to the "exotic" period

1

Cézanne was born on a cold winter's day in January 1839 in a house in the rue de l'Opéra, a peaceful street in Aix-en-Provence. It was, and still is, a street lined with delightful façades, some of which open into the courtyards of the numerous magnificent townhouses that grace the old city. Paul was the Cézanne family's first child. Soon after, the couple moved to 55 cours Mirabeau, where their hat business was situated. A second child, Marie, was born two years later, a sister with whom the painter would always have a warm and close relationship. Another daughter was born, but Paul never felt any real attachment to his second sister. It It should be acknowledged that every genius is first of all a child and before becoming the ill-mannered and often misunderstood adult that he was, Paul Cézanne experienced a studious and humdrum upbringing common to all middle-class boys of his era. Although this first period of the painter's life was a tranquil enough existence spent in one of France's most beautiful cities, he nevertheless made friends with an exceptional individual. From 1852 to 1858 Cézanne received a particularly thorough humanistic education at the Collège Bourbon, and one of his classmates and friends was Émile Zola, who was to have a decisive influence on his choice of career. Paul was an excellent pupil and first tried his hand at poetry, but, although Zola was enthusiastic about his efforts and tried to get him to take poetry seriously, Cézanne never really contemplated a literary career; despite his undoubted talent, literature was only a simple pastime. Cézanne and Zola had a friend in common, Jean-Baptiste Baille, who became a professor in the École Polytechnique, and the three youths were known as the "inseparables" around the "Collège". Like all romantically inclined youths of the time, they were never at a loss for things to debate and dreams to mull over, and this they did on their long walks in the local countryside fishing, swimming and hunting. Their ramblings sometimes took them in the direction of the Château de Galice or onto a wide plateau from which they could see the 'Tour de César' (Caesar's Tower). On longer expeditions, they got as far as the Carrière de Bibémus (Bibemus Quarry), from which the Romans once extracted the creamy

**Louis-Auguste Cézanne,
reading l'Évènement**
1866. Oil on canvas
200x120 cm
Washington
National Gallery of Art

pale stone to build ancient *Aquae Sextius* – the quarry to which Cézanne was to return so often to paint years later. The three friends also sometimes went to the Gorges d'Infernets, where Zola's father had built a dam, or scrambled up the slopes of Les Lauves. And here too, from this vantage point overlooking the town, Cézanne was later to return to paint, in this case the Mont Sainte-Victoire. Nevertheless, their favorite walk was usually to the village of Tholonet, and it was during these long carefree days of unauthorized absence from school that, unknowingly at the time, Cézanne was developing an adolescent passion for the landscapes that he was later to immortalize. Indeed a few years later, Zola wrote a fine and moving description of these fleeting moments: "There were three of us friends, three mischievous kids who were still grinding away at school work. On holidays and times when we could get away from study, we would go charging off at top speed into the country. We needed fresh air, sunshine, trails hidden in the depths of ravines, which we took over like conquerors [...]. In the winter we adored the cold, and the crisp echoing crunch of the frozen ground beneath our feet. We went off to eat omelettes in the surrounding villages [...]. In the summer our meeting place was always on the bank of the river, as we were obsessed with water." At that stage Cézanne was not known to have any particular predilection for painting. Although he won first prizes in a number of subjects throughout his school years, he only once received a commendation for drawing, a runner-up award. This was in the year when he went for drawing lessons at the Aix-en-Provence Art School. On the other hand, if there was no way of detecting signs of the future genius of modern art in Cézanne, what was well in evidence was his fiery, impetuous character and alternating bouts of rage and self-doubt. This difficult and devious character was to grow into a personality for whom the art of making enemies was commensurate with his talent.

Unfortunately, just as in the contemporary novels of Dickens, the days of childhood camaraderie had to end. The happy rambling through the Aix countryside was no more once Zola left for Paris in February 1858. Nevertheless, the separation of the two friends saw the beginning of a rich correspondence between them, in which they recalled their years of insouciance. Zola for his part was affected by this separation and made strenuous efforts to persuade his friend to move to Paris and become a painter. He could not at first get the better of Cézanne's indecisiveness and what was to prove his lifelong domination by his father. Once he had got his high school diploma, Cézanne enrolled as a student at the Aix Law Faculty, in conformity with his father's wishes, but eventually, as a result of his correspondence with Zola, he mustered the courage to claim his independence. He made out that he felt a calling to be an artist, but it was a claim motivated above all by a desire to meet up with his friend and by the lure

**Paul Cézanne
painting in his studio**
1905. Photo Émile Bernard
Paris
Musée d'Orsay

Still life
Sugar Bowl, Pears and blue Cup
1863/1865. Oil on canvas
30x41 cm
Aix-en-Provence
Musée Granet

of Paris. Cézanne's father's origins were in Aix and also in the Dauphiné region of eastern France; he was a hat-maker and then hat merchant by profession. He became a banker in 1847, and it was his rise in social status that was to confer upon his son a future free from economic worries. (Cézanne was eventually to say of him, "my father was a genius, he provided me with an annual income of 25 000 francs"). Nevertheless, at the time we are speaking of, an artistic career was not at all what this tight-fisted businessman had in mind for his son, for whom anything other than banking was out of the question. So Cézanne had to knuckle under and study law for two years, but in his spare time he continued to take refuge in writing poetry and drawing. He relived the pleasures of his secondary schooldays in the countryside, climbing Mont Sainte-Victoire, fishing in the river Arc, swimming, writing long letters to Zola. During the year following the start of Cézanne's law studies, his father celebrated the parvenu status that came with the success of his bank by buying what was to become one of the most potent features of the myth of Cézanne the painter. This was the property known as the Jas de Bouffan, a dilapidated summer residence that had once been occupied by the Governor of Provence during the pre-Revolutionary era, the *ancien régime*. It was a tall, imposing eighteenth-century building, set in grounds containing fine, mature trees. This vast house came to have the greatest importance for Cézanne, who throughout the very different periods of his career was happy to paint here far more than anywhere else. He quickly set about decorating the living room by creating the strange paintings that are now to be seen in the Petit Palais in Paris. On the top floor of the house, Cézanne eventually set up a studio with a view extending out over the vineyards and the hills of Les Lauves, but which in fact he seldom used because he found the tranquillity and light of the grounds so congenial. Cézanne was dispensed from doing his military service, as his father resorted to the well-known practice of paying another man to do it in his place, and so was free in 1859 to go to evening art classes. These were hold in the 'École municipale libre de dessin' in Aix, situated in the Musée Granet, and it was here that Cézanne was soon to be seen copying the works of the old masters. He practiced drawing in life classes at the school, and met up with former schoolmates from the Collège Bourbon, notably Achille Empéraire, a painter whose career was to be a succession of unmerited disappointments. The earliest photographs we have of Cézanne portray a young man of rather seductive appearance, with brown hair and large, dark, fiery eyes. Although extremely well educated, Cézanne was already exactly as everyone would describe him later: untidy, inarticulate in speech and uncouth in his manners. Thus it is no surprise that the future painter had little success with the fair sex during his youth.

Cézanne was increasingly neglecting his studies his time to devote to painting. A battle thus began to be fought, indirectly, between the father, who was still opposed to seeing his son leave, and on the other hand Zola, who knew how inclined to inertia his friend was and feared he might never move to Paris. The future author of *L'Assommoir* sent letter after letter to try to stiffen his friend's resolve: "Is painting nothing more to you than a whim that just came into your head one day when you were bored? Is it just a pastime, something to talk about, an excuse for not getting on with your law studies? Well, if it is, I can understand the way you are behaving; you're right not to push things too far, and to avoid family problems for yourself. But if painting is really your vocation (and that's how I have always seen it), and if you feel you can achieve something after working hard at it, then you are a mystery to me, a sphinx, something incomprehensible and obscure. Do you want me to be frank? Don't take it badly, but you lack strength of character; you dread fatigue in any shape or form, in thought as well as in deed; your guiding principle in life is to drift with the tide and let yourself be controlled by time and chance. If I were in your place, I would want to have a say in the matter and take my fate in my hands despite the risks, not vacillate between two such different futures, painting and the lawcourts. I feel sorry for you, because this dithering must cause you a lot of pain, and if it was me it would be one more good reason for tearing open the veil; one thing or the other, definitely be a lawyer, or definitely be an artist. But don't remain something without a name, wearing a lawyer's robe smeared with paint." Faced with such a powerful harangue, Cézanne could not do other than take stock of his situation: painting was indeed his destiny. When further resistance was clearly impossible, Cézanne's father reluctantly gave in.

So Paul Cézanne set off for Paris in April 1861 with all the high hopes of youth. Zola was delighted to meet up with the friend who had shared his dreamy adolescence in Aix and had already drafted a rigorous timetable of activities that could not fail to turn him into the painter of the century. "From six till eleven o'clock you will go to a life class; then lunch, followed from noon till four by a session at the Louvre or the Luxembourg, copying a masterwork of your choice". In fact, once he got to Paris, Cézanne began by receiving advice by a fellow southerner, Villevieille, but he was soon put off by the latter's mediocrity as a painter. He became a regular attender at the Académie Suisse, a studio where students could follow life classes for ten francs a month. Cézanne met Achille Empéraire there and also made the acquaintance of Monet, Guillaumin, Renoir, and notably Camille Pissarro, with whom he was later to paint out of doors. So he led a somewhat lonely and anonymous life, forcing himself – no easy task – to accept the unwelcome discipline inherent in the painter's apprenticeship: his twin ambitions were to gain admission to the École des Beaux-Arts

Portrait of Achille Emperaire
1867/1870. Oil on canvas
200x122 cm
Paris
Musée d'Orsay

and have pictures accepted for exhibit at the annual Paris Salon. Until this time his experience of art extended little further than the paintings to be seen in the Aix-en-Provence churches and the Musée Granet, so he now became a regular visitor to the Louvre, where he applied himself to copying works by the great masters. Soon he also began to be familiar with the work of contemporary masters such as Courbet and Manet, but his fellow students at the Académie Suisse were insensitive to the originality of his drawings and kept their distance from him somewhat, with the result that Cézanne had the feeling of being an outsider. As he put it in a letter to a friend back in Aix: "I get by more or less [...] But you mustn't think I'll become a Parisian." Being aware of Cézanne's failure to fit in and growing feeling of discouragement, Zola looked for a way to persuade him to stay on in Paris and so one day asked him to paint his portrait. Cézanne accepted reluctantly but was so displeased with the result that he slashed the canvas. In truth Cézanne throughout his life was rarely satisfied with his work; it frequently happened that he was furious with his inability to translate his vision into reality and ended up destroying canvases. When he failed to gain admission to the Beaux-Arts, his hopes of success in Paris were crushed and he decided to leave. In September 1861 he returned to Aix.

Thus, the disillusioned Cézanne began working in his father's bank, work for which he had nothing but distaste, though at least he was free to paint in the tranquillity of the Jas de Bouffan. Yet despite the peacefulness and harmony of his life in this retreat, he very quickly became aware that life is full of inconsistencies: he had hardly returned to his father's bank before he was longing to go back to Paris. Uncertainty about his vocation had turned into a firm resolve without his really having been aware of it. It was at this time that he wrote a sly couplet in a ledger: "Cézanne the banker does not see without fear / Behind his desk a young painter appear" . His father was as hostile as ever to this career but philosophical about its inevitability, and so allowed his son to return to Paris in November 1862. But in return for a monthly allowance of 125 francs, which would allow Paul to dedicate himself to his art studies without economic problems, he made it clear that he expected completely satisfactory results from the Beaux-Arts, as this was the institution that counted in French artistic life. Every career worth having depended on it and on the Annual Exhibition ('Salon') that was associated with it. Unfortunately, once again things were never going to be easy, and the worthy Monsieur Cézanne's expectations were destined to be disappointed yet again. As soon as he returned to Paris, Paul was promptly turned down by the Beaux-Arts with the following verdict, "Cézanne has the temperament of a colorist, but he exaggerates" – an ironic assessment in view of the unanimous recognition of his work after his death. Yet Cézanne took no offence, as he had few illusions about such a hidebound and

reactionary institution. Those who ran the Beaux-Arts were disciples of Ingres, whose impeccably accurate draftsmanship and precedence of line over color were the officially recommended style. In addition to which, landscapes as subjects in themselves were despised, as opposed to settings for historical or mythological subjects. There could be no meeting halfway. What was required could not be other than unacceptable to Cézanne with his taste for the real world and the expression of the artist's personality: for him the artist should always stand out by refusing to accept compromises, whether social or artistic. Cézanne was making great efforts at this time to discipline himself, but his inflexibility, which has been much discussed, was nothing more than the reaction of a misunderstood genius to the narrow-minded conventions of contemporary society. His hatred of imposture and bourgeois posing was so pronounced that one day when he saw Manet all dandified to impress his café devotees, he refused to shake his hand on the pretext that he had not washed at all that day.

Cézanne was delighted to have squeezed cash and freedom out of his father, and so became a regular student at the Académie Suisse, where, in contrast to

Head of an old man
1866. Oil on canvas
51x48 cm
Paris
Musée d'Orsay

The Lawyer
Uncle Dominique
1866. Oil on canvas
65x54 cm
Paris
Musée d'Orsay

the old fogies of the Beaux-Arts, they championed realism. He became involved in the lively debates in cafés about different tendencies in art, notably the Café Guerbois where in 1867 Monet conceived the idea of an independent group exhibition, once it became clear that certain painters could expect no support from the official Paris Salon. Cézanne felt completely at home in the conflict between the pedantic eclecticism of the official circles and the realism of the modern school incarnated by Manet and Courbet. He was in Zola's company in 1863 when he visited the exhibition of paintings rejected by the Paris "Salon des Refusés". He was overwhelmed by Manet's *Déjeuner sur l'herbe* ('Lunch on the Grass'), which because of its parodic and iconoclastic tone as well as its definitely modern painterly style was to become the source of several of Cézanne's compositions in the years ahead. In addition to pictures repeating the title of Manet's work, there are other series of works that were directly inspired by it, such as the *Pastorale ou Idylle*. Here too, we find the same principal theme that is found in Manet's work and which outraged the pious establishment of the time, namely daring to portray nudity outside a mythological or historical context. Put simply, if a woman who is disporting herself nude in the open air is not a goddess, the only other thing she can be is a shameless hussy. In any case, just as with Manet, the men in modern clothes sitting nonchalantly on the grass make it clear that the theme is certainly not borrowed from elegiac poetry. Furthermore, Cézanne took the opportunity to portray himself in this picture in the shape of the man lying alongside the water. He translated this fantasy-like vision via thickly painted brushwork in bright and dark colors at the same time, using heavy and starkly juxtaposed masses. This scene of relaxation alongside water is in fact the first of the many bathing scenes that Cézanne went on to paint. At this time Manet was undeniably his principal contemporary source of inspiration, but the young man was also impressed by Delacroix, and above all Courbet. The latter inspired Cézanne until 1870, who found in his work traces of the somber painting of Ribera and the great Spanish masters. A mind as subtle as Matisse's perfectly understood how an excessive adulation of Courbet's work could hold Cézanne back: "Cézanne did not need to fear being influenced by Poussin, because he was certain not to copy the exterior form of Poussin's work, whereas when he was affected by Courbet, just like the other painters of his time, his work was impregnated with Courbet's influence and his expression was limited by it". The supple, bold technique of the *Sugar bowl, pears and blue cup* is a good example of this influence in the still life genre.

But being an inveterate Southerner like Zola, Cézanne rarely remained for more than six months in Paris (where he frequently changed his address: rue des Feuillantines, rue Beautreillis, and rue Notre-Dame-des-Champs). He often retreated to the tranquillity of the Jas de Bouffan, and until 1870 he regularly

spent part of the year in Aix, where his uncle Dominique and his father were models for several portraits of extraordinary strength and intensity. In *Louis-Auguste Cézanne reading L'Événement*, a powerful work executed with the palette knife, reality is entirely reconstituted, from the psychology of the sitter to the setting in which he is placed (on the wall above his head is one of his son's still lifes, as if it were a perfectly normal object in this very bourgeois home). Contrarily to what was the case, Cézanne's father appears to be a kind man and his son shows him reading *L'Événement*, which would certainly not have been his normal newspaper. This was in fact the paper in which Zola published articles championing the new generation of artists and violently attacked the committee of the annual Salon. Far from approving of this kind of militancy, the father considered Salon-approved painting to be the only permissible type: perhaps unconsciously and touchingly this painting reflects Cézanne's fervent desire for paternal recognition, a desire which was destined, alas, to remain unsatisfied. *The Lawyer (Uncle Dominique)* is one of many portraits of Cézanne's maternal uncle, M. Aubert. He is dressed as a lawyer. On other occasions Cézanne portrayed him in different guises, for example as a monk or an Arab. In this remarkably powerful portrait that fills the canvas, Cézanne worked with a palette knife, embedding line and detail into thick layers of paint. The sitter's hands are particularly fine and expressive, like those of a Christ giving a blessing rather than of a humble (and fake) lawyer. Likewise the *Head of an Old Man* is striking for its violent contrasts and the vigor of the youthful works.

As a major proof of the way in which Cézanne's style was developing, the

Portrait of Achille Emperaire
1869/1870. Charcoal on paper
49x31 cm
Paris
Louvre, D.A.G. (fonds Orsay)

Portrait of Achille Emperaire was painted a few years after the portrait of Cézanne's father reading *L'Événement* and the painter sent this astonishing picture to the 1870 Salon in a mood of puzzling optimism. As usual, he was rewarded with a brutal rejection, as the selection committee saw it not so much as an indirect homage to the artists of the Spanish Golden Age and the daring yet poignant canvases of Velazquez but as a blasphemous defiance of the technical and aesthetic canons governing "official" art. A caustic article on the Salon was illustrated by a venomous caricature of Cézanne and his rejected canvases. Cézanne was never one to accept attacks meekly and replied: "Yes, my dear sir, I paint how I see, how I feel [...] and I have very strong feelings. Other people also feel and see as I do, but they do not dare. [...] Well, I dare, I dare, my good man. [...] I have the courage of my opinions, and he laughs best who laughs last!" After this there could be no going back, and the gulf of misunderstanding between Cézanne and the world of official art was thereafter permanent and unbridgeable and made even deeper by many a malevolent attack upon him. Only a few years separate the portraits of Cézanne's father and of Emperaire, but the evolution in style and technique is apparent. Whereas in the father's portrait the decorative motifs were handled in an illusionist manner, in the Emperaire portrait they are treated with great economy of means and virtually schematic. This economy of means is emphasized by the accuracy of the patches of color and the evenness of the lighting. The artist was beginning his long quest for an understanding of the structure and essence of things, in order to get away from the illusionism that had characterized painting in the past, when the painter's task was to try to capture the mirage of a three-dimensional world on a two-dimensional canvas. Emperaire was a hunch-backed dwarf who lived in extreme poverty and failed to make any impact as a painter during his life. Cézanne helped him as best he could, and after the Franco-Prussian War (ca. 1870) in a surge of generosity he had Emperaire move in with him in his apartment in rue de Jussieu. But the latter soon moved out, such was the strain of living with Cézanne. Yet in the year when the portrait was painted, relations between the two friends were still excellent, and this work remains one of the milestones in the first period of Cézanne's art. The striking frontal pose, which seems to herald the coming abandonment of traditional perspective, confers great dignity on the sitter. It is a sign of the friendship between him and the artist and of the great respect that Cézanne felt for this human being, the victim of a caprice of nature in having a noble soul and the head of a Spanish grandee above the deformed body of a court jester. The *Portrait of Achille Emperaire*, this time via the meticulous detail that is possible with drawing, is less dramatic but perhaps truer to life in conveying the melancholy and wounded intelligence of the sitter.

At the same time as portraits, Cézanne was doing a lot of still life painting. The *Still Life with Coffeepot* is a fine example of this genre in which the artist expressed himself throughout his life. It is clearly difficult, as was noted by various commentators at the time, Zola among them, not to see here the influence of those Spanish still life paintings that Cézanne admired on his afternoons in the Louvre after his morning studies at the Académie Suisse. We see the same everyday objects that we find in the work of the eighteenth-century painter and engraver Ribera, who used a range of somber colors, as well as the dark backgrounds so popular with Courbet. Like the latter, Cézanne painted wide patches of very contrasting color to convey the effect of light. But still life is not the ideal genre in which to express passion, and this was a time when Cézanne had much fear and anguish that he needed to exteriorize. Generally speaking, those early paintings of Cézanne that incorporate human figures are really visions of love or of mayhem dredged up from a subconscious filled with repressed urges. They are outlets for numerous fantasies captured in horrific pictures going through the full range of depraved activity: rape, abduction, witches' sabbath, murder (*The Strangled Woman*), subjects taken straight out of Romantic literature. It was at this time that Cézanne gave expression to that side of his character that was turbulent and passionate, driven by uncontrollable impulse and angst; this style he termed *couillard*, a rare slang word meaning "having big testicles". These pictures with striking light effects, illustrating morbid and erotic subjects, were genre paintings inspired stylistically by the Spanish and Italian masters. A particularly good example is *the Magdalen or Sorrow* in which he used a powerful chiaroscuro effect to create an appropriate dramatic atmosphere. In imitation of Manet, Cézanne used thick layers of paint that he shaped with a brush which was to become Van Gogh's method. Mary Magdalen, the very incarnation of remorse and suffering, is handled in a sinuous way, creating a slightly baroque effect. Partly as a result of his fascination with Baudelaire's poetry, Cézanne's fondness for the theme of the death's head can be found in other works of his youth, but the idea of death was to become an obsession much later, during the 1890s.

However at this time, looking to the example of Manet, Cézanne still had the ambition of creating more "neutral", large-scale works containing a number of human figures, which could conceivably be submitted for the Salon's approval. The fact is that despite his clear negative view of official institutions, Cézanne had few illusions about his chances of success outside the official "circuit" .

Gray pitcher owned by Paul Cézanne
Paris
Musée d'Orsay

Still life with coffeepot
1869.Oil on canvas
64x81 cm
Paris
Musée d'Orsay

The strangled woman
1870/1872. Oil on canvas
31x25 cm
Paris
Musée d'Orsay

So he stubbornly persisted in submitting pictures to the selection committee, and over the years this became almost a joke. Few of the pictures intended to get him into the Salon were in fact completed. A good example is *Paul Alexis reading to Emile Zola*, a fine and substantial picture in which many of Manet's traits can be detected in the overall composition and the monochrome expanses of sober color. Another son of Aix, Paul Alexis, arrived in Paris at the end of the 1860s, became a poet and novelist, and then went on to publish the first biography of his friend Zola in 1882. The painting no doubt depicts Alexis reading one of his works in Zola's house in Aix. From 1869 onwards Cézanne cohabited with a girl whom he first met when she was working as an artist's model in Paris. This was Hortense Fiquet, from the Jura in eastern France. Eleven years his junior and a bookbinder by trade, she was destined to be the only woman in his life, but it was to be a shared life somewhat devoid of love rather than a fine and enduring romance. Hortense was for Cézanne what Marthe would be for Bonnard a few years later, a model. Cézanne was in Aix in 1870 when the Franco-Prussian War broke out, but he remained blithely indifferent to it. At first he hid at the Jas de Bouffan, but when the gendarmes came looking for him, he fled into the countryside and his mother let them search the house in vain. Without the slightest qualms of conscience, he went to live on the coast at L'Estaque, where his mother had rented a fisherman's house. From his earliest childhood years he had spent a lot of time in this handsome village close to Marseille, and this was where he happily spent his time painting, quite simply ignoring his call-up papers and as indifferent as ever to political matters. By contrast, his friend Bazille, also a painter, volunteered for service and was killed in battle at the age of twenty-nine. Writing of this period later, Cézanne commented: "During the war I did a lot of painting in the open air at L'Estaque. But I have nothing exceptional to report about 1870/71. I divided my time between landscapes and studio work." This was in a letter to the famous art dealer Ambroise Vollard, who was also an author and publisher, and who played a crucial role in the history of painting in organizing the first exhibitions of the modernist masters. On returning from Paris, Cézanne decided to devote himself exclusively to landscape painting, but at first he limited himself to sketches and studies, and his substantial work on natural subjects did not really begin until he reached L'Estaque. This setting concludes off the first half of the artist's career, a development that reached creative fruition in the bountiful years of the 1880s.

When the Republic was proclaimed, Cézanne, no doubt reluctantly, was appointed to the commission supervising both the art school and the museum of Aix, presumably because his father was a local worthy and wished his son to climb the same social ladder. But yet again Cézanne had no interest in public affairs, continuing to devote himself to landscapes, all the more enthusiastical-

The Poet's Dream
1859/1860. Oil on canvas
82x66 cm
Aix-en-Provence
Musée Granet

The Magdalen, or Sorrow
1868/1869. Oil on canvas
165x125 cm
Paris
Musée d'Orsay

ly as painting outside in the country was an exhilarating experience after the confinement of the studio or copying paintings in museums. After the frustrations caused by artistic as well as human rejection in Paris, Cézanne made the definitive choice of the countryside and landscape painting as opposed to urban environments. This was the key turning point when the pictorial language of Cézanne's youth gave way to a tranquillity and an unprecedented mood of humility in contemplation of the infinite diversity of subjects to be found in nature. Enthralled by landscape, Cézanne now began to paint exclusively in the open air, and forced himself for the first time to record solely what his eye saw. The subject was no longer the product of his imagination but reality as he observed it.

Paul Alexis reading to Emile Zola
1869/1870. Oil on canvas
130x160 cm
São Paulo
Museu de Arte

2

Pontoise and Auvers: the contact with impressionism

It seems that for five years Cézanne did not set foot in L'Estaque. After the war, partly to return to the heart of contemporary artistic life, but also to prevent his irascible father finding out about his domestic arrangements, Cézanne and his concubine returned to Paris. They were soon beset by financial problems. Contrary to what one might have hoped, this shared existence brought little relief from the artist's loneliness or from his morbid distrust of other people. In fact, if anything, things worsened, as Cézanne now had to provide for a family. His despondency deepened through quarrels because of his intransigence with almost all of his friends, the fellow Aixois Solari and Zola first and foremost. Despite many ups and downs, Zola was nevertheless to remain for a good number of years a person who was close to Cézanne amid his domestic problems and his depressive moods. Yet the two friends had to avoid talking about art any more: their views were now too divergent, and Zola was of no help to the artist in this area. It was at this time of profound crisis that Camille Pissarro invited Cézanne to visit him at Pontoise in the Oise valley, a place where Charles-François Daubigny had once lived. Being familiar with the patient, easy-going personality of Pissarro, Cézanne, despite his normally mistrustful character, accepted this invitation with relief. Apart from the need for a change of air and to be able to find peace on his own in the soothing calm of the countryside once more, he hoped he might improve his technique by being with Pissarro, nine years his elder. For his part, Pissarro, who sincerely believed in the genius of Cézanne, assumed the role of master from 1872 to 1873. He did this not like Manet from a distance and only by virtue of his painting but directly by means of judicious advice. Pissarro in fact enabled Cézanne to free himself from his somber and theatrical early style and assimilate the discoveries of the Impressionists. The emotional rebelliousness of Cézanne was going to meet more than its match in the revolutionary yet mature mind of Pissarro. The latter had this to say: "There is hope for our Cézanne, and I've seen here a way of painting of remarkable force and vigor. If, as I hope, he stays some time in Auvers, where he's going to live, he'll surprise many an artist who has written

Flowers in Delft vase
1873. Oil on canvas
41 x 27 cm
Paris
Musée d'Orsay

**Paul Cézanne engraving
beside Dr Gachet**
1872/1873. Pencil on paper
20x13 cm
Paris
Louvre, D.A.G. (fonds Orsay)

**Camille Pissaro,
Self-Portrait with soft hat**
1874. Charcoal on paper
24,2x13 cm
Paris
Louvre, D.A.G. (fonds Orsay)

Portrait of Dr Gachet
1872/1873. Charcoal stumped
on paper
32x21 cm
Paris
Louvre, D.A.G. (fonds Orsay)

him off too soon." In the hazy, subdued landscapes of the Ile-de-France, which the Impressionists were so fond of, a whole range of motifs was available to open-air painters. The two of them frequently went off to paint directly from nature, side by side, (*Pissarro setting off to paint, Portrait of Camille Pissarro*) and Cézanne even went as far as to copy one of Pissarro's pictures meticulously in order to familiarize himself with his technique. In return it must be said that Pissarro gained from the contact with Cézanne, with his paintings acquiring a firmer structure. Pissarro criticized Cézanne's violent outlines and his unmodulated flat expanses of paint laid on with the palette knife, and persuaded him to think more about achieving a gradation of tones with linear contours. He also managed in some measure to get him to apply paint with small touches of the brush, which is how we see the flowers painted in *Flowers in Delft Vase*, and to rid his palette of dark colors and work only with primaries and their derivatives. A bright palette and tiny brush strokes: these were thus the two main recommendations. As for the more subjective side of things, Pissarro also urged

Pissaro setting off to paint

1874/1877. Pencil

19x11 cm

Paris

Louvre, D.A.G. (fonds Orsay)

Portrait of Camille Pissaro

1874/1877. Pencil

13x10 cm

Paris

Louvre, D.A.G. (fonds Orsay)

Cézanne to paint only what he saw, to observe nature objectively without involving his own interpretation: a painter must be nothing more than an objective observer. This could only distance Cézanne from the wild fantasies that haunted some of the painting of his early period. Cézanne learnt to apply tones while scrupulously observing the reflection of colors according to their surroundings, thus creating for the whole composition a much more harmonious atmosphere. He also began to take much more careful note of aerial perspective, from the foreground to the horizon. Cézanne benefited from the contact with Pissarro not just stylistically, he also had the advantage of meeting another admirer, DR. Gachet, who was a talented and original man, interested in everything new. A socialist and practitioner of homeopathy in its infancy, Gachet was happy to accept canvases from patients unable to pay his fees. He had the luck to acquire work from patients whose paintings were later to grace the walls of museums. Gachet was an admirer of Courbet and frequented avant-garde haunts in Paris, as well as being an amateur painter himself. He also had a house at Auvers-sur-Oise, not far from Pontoise. Two of Cézanne's drawings have left us with a likeness of this man, who was one of the first to believe in his genius. *The Portrait of DR. Gachet* depicts the "good doctor" in part profile smoking a pipe and wearing a cap. It is anything but a flattering interpretation of the sort expected by so many collectors and wealthy patrons eager to have their artistic good taste appreciated, but rather a good-natured, intimate portrait of the man known as "DR. Saffron" , because of the color of his hair. In *Cézanne engraving beside DR. Gachet*, Cézanne has placed himself into a domestic sketch with DR. Gachet with pipe and cap once again. It was in fact Gachet who taught Cézanne to engrave. For the first time, apart from Pissarro ("like a father to me, rather like the good Lord" was how Cézanne viewed the latter), someone was interested in his painting, and he always felt at home in the company of Gachet and his wife. The Doctor managed to persuade Cézanne, who was living with his family in a hotel near Pissarro's house, to come and live with him in Auvers. From the end of 1872 to the spring of 1874, in these even calmer rural surroundings than Pontoise, Cézanne was able to study the changing aspects of nature in a mild, temperate climate. Of course one of the very first subjects he painted was *DR. Gachet's House*. Cézanne's composition of this painting was similar to a technique borrowed by Pissarro from Corot and from photography, in that he used prominent diverging lines of perspective to make a strong link between the foreground and the background (the same strategy as used in *Village Road in Auvers)*. This winter scene painted in cold, muted colors shows just how resistant Cézanne's art was, despite Pissarro's teaching, to the principles of Impressionism, a style requiring essentially a naturalist vision and the dissolution of forms in space. In this picture, with its firmly

The Hanged Man's House
1873. Oil on canvas
55x66 cm
Paris
Musée d'Orsay

Crossroad
of the rue Rémy in Auvers
1873. Oil on canvas
38x45 cm
Paris
Musée d'Orsay

Village road in Auvers

1872/1873. Oil on canvas
46x55 cm
Paris
Musée d'Orsay

defined masses (particularly the centrally positioned gable-end wall), Cézanne remained faithful above all to a notion of structure and substance. Any perception of objects that he might have was in fact much more complex than that of the Impressionists, and their technique was never for him more than a point of departure. This is made strikingly obvious by a comparison of landscapes painted at this time. Cézanne was in a relaxed mood (Hortense had just borne his son Paul in January 1872) in the company of Van Gogh, Guillaumin (an Impressionist friend of Monet and Pissarro who painted fine Creuse landscapes) and Doctor Gachet. Enjoying a period of relative serenity, he put his time to good use and tirelessly painted Auvers landscapes. Intent on capturing his wealth of observations accurately on canvas, he reworked them over and over again, never able to call a halt. In *Crossroad of the rue Rémy in Auvers*, Cézanne has abandoned the neutrality of black and white and his treatment

Dr. Gachet's house in Auvers
1872/1873. Oil on canvas
46x38 cm
Paris
Musée d'Orsay

has become lighter. His palette is brighter and his sky captures something of the luminosity of the Impressionists while yet remaining radically different because of his brushwork. Cézanne applies his paint with broad, vigorous strokes and creates a powerful image of a landscape. His sky is painted with dabs of paint juxtaposed alongside one another to recreate the subject without containing it in any *a priori* sort of way. And yet amid this sophisticated composition, centering on the volumes of the houses (roofs and gables), the different features of the picture retain their material distinctiveness. The earth, the stones of the houses and the vegetation do not evaporate in an atmospheric haze but stand out starkly in all their truth and individuality. What we are looking at is the result of a long process of composition as much as at a recording, and Cézanne's own words must be kept in mind: "In the painter there are two things: the eye and the brain and they must work together and help one another: you have to work at their mutual development; of the eye by looking at things, of the brain by the logic of organized sensations, which provides the means of expression." Thus the building up of layers of paint reflects the long process involved in the making of a composition. Cézanne compared the areas of his painted canvas to the stylized colored motifs of a playing card and by rejecting the reductive vision of impressionism he defined the principles of painting for future generations. He wanted in fact to attribute the same importance to perception with the eye as to the working out of an independent pictorial system. In *The Hanged Man's house,* (a house so named because its owner had committed suicide) we can once again see how much Cézanne had assimilated impressionism in the light and subtle tones of the picture, while still stopping short of a complete adoption of its techniques. This key work, which marks the end of his *couillard* ("testicular"!, i.e erotico-fantastical) period, derives its vibrancy from the broad panorama over the countryside in the central upper half of the canvas. As distinct from Pissarro's foregrounds, in which perspective leads the eye in a particular direction (a technique that Cézanne had borrowed in *Dr. Gachet's House* and *Village Road in Auvers*) the foreground in this picture is composed in an irregular way. There is no specific viewpoint but rather a number of interrupted lines of vision and the priority given to structure and mass contrasts with the rather more random composition of Pissarro's canvases. In this particular instance, the wall coming in to the bottom left of the picture seems almost intended to halt the eye's movement. Compared with Pissarro's and the other Impressionists' pictures, a landscape like this one seems much more deliberately constructed, infinitely more material and concrete. Independent from the issue of composition, it was also at this time that Cézanne began to give a sense of structure to the surface of his canvases by means of his brushwork, specifically diagonal brushstrokes. As we can

A Modern Olympia

1873/1874. Oil on canvas
46x55 cm
Paris
Musée d'Orsay

Bathsheba
1875/1877. Oil on canvas
29x25 cm
Aix-en-Provence
Musée Granet

A Lunch on Grass
c. 1873/1875. Oil on canvas
21x27 cm
Paris
Musée de l'Orangerie

just detect beneath the surface of the vegetation on the left, he tackled the biggest surfaces by covering the canvas with longish brushstrokes making up a network of oblique hatching. Cézanne applied the light brushstroke technique learnt from Pissarro but modified it in his own fashion. Hence thick strokes in relief to depict compact objects picked out by the light and little dabs with the brush for example to create the effect of vegetation and its varied tones. An exceptional circumstance about this picture is that it was exhibited twice during the artist's lifetime, at the centennial of French art in 1889 and the exhibition of the "XX" group in Brussels in 1890. At this time Cézanne was eking out a precarious existence on the allowance provided by his father and still could not count on acceptance by the Salon selection committee, which would have boosted sales of his pictures. But he made an acquaintance that at least spared him the cost of buying his materials. Once again through Pissarro, Cézanne came into contact not only with Paul Durand-Ruel, the first dealer in Impressionist paintings, but in 1873 he met the man who was to become one of his best friends, the famous "Père Tanguy" (Father Tanguy). An artists' colorman from Brittany, Tanguy had an almost supernatural instinct for detecting quality in art, thanks to which he came to know not only Pissarro but also Gauguin, Signac, Sisley, Van Gogh and Seurat, assisting them economically by accepting paintings in payment for paint and canvases. These other "modern" painters were no better off than Cézanne, and it was perhaps this shared adversity, rather than any common artistic ground as regards style, that for a long time united Cézanne with the new generation of artists. Cézanne's ties with impressionism resulted above all from his admiration for the work of the leader of the movement, Manet, (to the extent of borrowing one of his major titles and themes, *Le Déjeuner sur l'herbe*) and from his friendship with Pissarro and to a lesser extent Monet and Renoir. This young group of painters was first known as the "Batignolles Group" between 1869 and 1875 when they met in the Café Guerbois, at 2 Grand-Rue des Batignolles (now Avenue de Clichy). When their work was still rejected after 1870 by the authorities of the Third Republic, they decided to go ahead with an independent exhibition, the idea for which had first been mooted by Monet. Cézanne shared their desire to exhibit independently, and Pissarro invited him to take part once he had overcome the opposition of certain members of the group who feared that Cézanne's harsh style might damage their image. The group gave itself the title *'Limited Company of Painters, Sculptors and Engravers'* and ran its exhibition for a month from 15 April 1874 in the studios of the photographer Nadar on Boulevard des Capucines. As is well known, it was torn apart by critics and public alike, with Cézanne as the number one target. His *A Modern Olympia*, inspired by Manet's *Olympia*, which had caused a scandal at the 1865 Salon, was particularly attacked by the more conservative critics. They were outraged at the blatant depiction of an aspect of social reality, prostitution, that the prim and proper wanted to keep well hidden. A far cry from the cold and clinical nudity of Manet's picture, Cézanne's in fact shows a realistic vision of a naked prostitute being lusted after by her client in an opium-like haze. Whereas Manet painted the "after", Cézanne depicts the "before", the moment when the prostitute is being displayed to the client by her maid. On the other hand, the cat in Manet's picture, which incarnates evil, is now replaced by a ridiculous little dog. The origin of this work is in fact interesting. One day in 1873, when Cézanne was with his friends, conversation came round to the subject of Manet's picture and Cézanne's first version of *A Modern Olympia*, dating back to 1869. The painter made a second version, in which he also placed himself seen from the back. It is subtly ironic and lacks the stiffness of the earlier version. Painted at great speed by Cézanne's normal standards, the picture almost gives the impression of being a preliminary sketch, and its pastel tones make it a much more suave version than the first. *A Modern Olympia* clearly shows that although the techniques of the Impressionists helped Cézanne to "discipline" his themes, they were still dredged up from obscure regions of his subconscious. Love could never be serene, nor could experience be life-enhancing; above all woman was essentially demonic and totally identified with sexuality (*Nude Woman with a Mirror*). We see this in *The Temptation of Saint Anthony*, in which, metaphorically, Cézanne

Nude woman with a mirror
c. 1872. Oil on canvas
17x22 cm
Aix-en-Provence
Musée Granet

portrays himself tormented by unsated desires. This version is the third and last variation by Cézanne on this theme, which has been painted since the Middle Ages. Hortense was certainly the model for the voluptuous woman who heralds the looming theme of the bathers, when all anecdotal framework will be dispensed with and anonymous nudes will be depicted in a timeless setting. DR. Gachet bought the second version of *A Modern Olympia*, and thus Cézanne made his first sale. The critics, naturally, did not share this faith in Cézanne's talent, and countless acid comments of the following sort were made: "Last Sunday the public expressed its disgust before the spectacle of a fantastic figure being offered to an opium addict beneath an opium sky. This apparition of pink flesh, offered like a lustful vision by a sort of demon on a celestial cloud, this corner of artificial paradise, stunned even the hardened onlooker. Cézanne makes one suspect that he is a sort of madman who paints in a state of delirium tremens." But the artist no longer attached much importance to other people's opinions, and it is significant that in exhibiting Olympia and refusing to espouse a strictly naturalist vision, he was demonstrating the distance that existed between him and the Impressionist movement. Nevertheless he did manage to sell a picture, the famous *The Hanged Man'house in Auvers*. It was bought for 300 francs by Count Doria, the enlightened patron of the arts who was to support Stanislas Lépine. However, the end of exhibition accounts showed that the undertaking had been a failure and each participant had to make a financial contribution. The consequence for Cézanne was that in May 1874 he had to return home to ask his father for more money. Louis-Auguste Cézanne took the view that Paul had disappointed him in every respect, and he was more hostile to him than ever. Only his mother showed him tenderness and understanding, and the artist reciprocated her affection, going so far as to devote a whole room in his apartment to her souvenirs later on (only to see the sanctuary wrecked by Hortense in a fit of jealousy). After the Franco-Prussian War (1870), Cézanne's father retired from banking, and apportioned his fortune to his son and two daughters in advance to reduce the eventual death duties that would have to be paid. He still administered his estate in authoritarian fashion, and his children were not free to do what they wished with it. A fine self-portrait executed around 1875 (Self-*portrait with Rose Background*) shows us what the artist looked like in his prime. It is an astonishingly powerful image of a man who has thus far always refused to compromise and has now become too old to change. This same characteristic emerges from other Cézanne self-portraits, abundant in defiance and passion, such as *Portrait of the Artist*, where, in the same three-quarter pose, his bitterness and misanthropy are apparent.

Portrait of the Artist
1877/1880. Oil on canvas
25,5x14,5 cm
Paris
Musée d'Orsay

**Self-Portrait
with rose background**
c. 1875. Oil on canvas
66x55 cm
France
Private Collection

The Temptation of St Anthony
1875. Oil on canvas
47x56 cm
Paris
Musée d'Orsay

Following pages:

Portrait of Paul Cézanne
1875.
Aix-en-Provence
Musée Granet

Portrait of the Artist
1873/1874. Oil on canvas
64x53 cm
Paris
Musée d'Orsay

For financial reasons, instead of a new collective exhibition that could well prove a risky venture, the Batignolles Group held a sale in 1875 in the Drouot auction rooms, but it too was a failure. Nevertheless, via Renoir it enabled Cézanne to make the acquaintance of Victor Choquet. Just like Père Tanguy and Doctor Gachet before him, he was to become one of his best friends. Despite his profession of customs officer, he was a collector with impeccably sure and independent taste. He was one of the first patrons of the Impressionists, whose work he discovered at the sale on 24 March 1875. Like Cézanne, he was a fervent admirer of Delacroix, and owned almost twenty of his paintings, as well as works by Manet and Courbet. Henceforth he was a personal benefactor watching over Cézanne, offering him support amid the climate of general hostility. It was not long before Cézanne made a summer visit to L'Estaque to paint for him, commissioned to do seascapes and views around the Gulf of Marseille. In a letter to Pissarro (2 July 1876), he had this to say: "I left Aix a month ago and I've started painting what Monsieur Choquet asked for, two small pictures with the sea in the background. It's like a playing card here. Red roofs against a blue sea. If the weather is fine, I might be able to complete them. For the moment I haven't done anything. But some subjects need three or four months, which is fine because the vegetation does not change. The olivetrees and the pines are always green. The sunlight is so powerful that objects seem to me to turn into silhouettes, not just in black and white, but in blue, red, brown, and purple. I may be wrong but it seems to me that this is the exact opposite of three-dimensional relief. How happy our Auvers people would be here, painting their landscapes [...] If I can, I'll stay at least a month in this place, because the subject deserves at least two-meter canvases..."

The Roofs
1877. Pencil and watercolor
47x59 cm
Bern
Hahnoser Collection

**Landscape with red roof
(Pinetree in l'Estaque)**
1876. Oil on canvas
73x60 cm
Paris
Musée d'Orsay

Still life with Soup Tureen
1877. Oil on canvas
65x81 cm
Paris
Musée d'Orsay

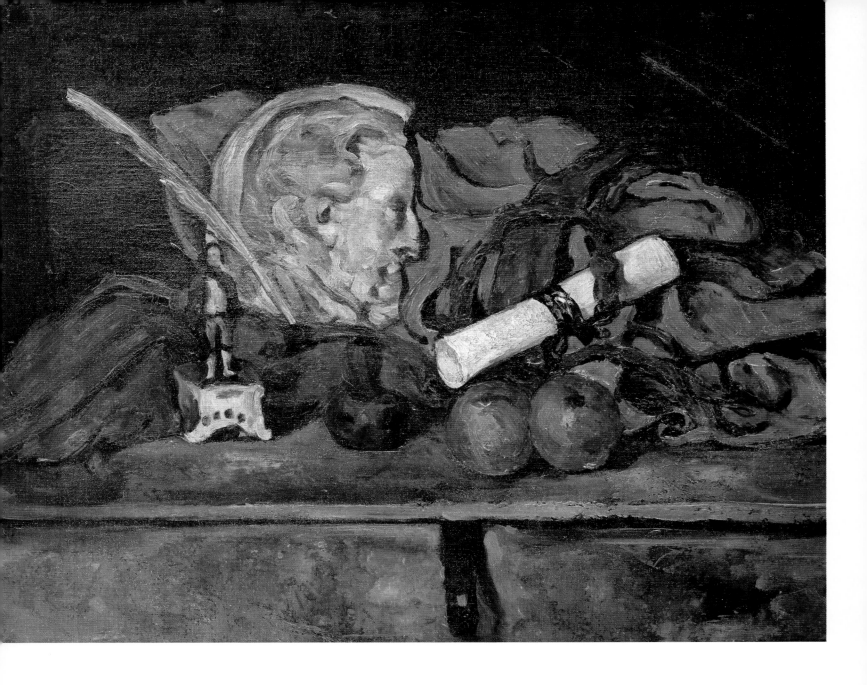

**Still life with medallion
of Philippe Solari**
1873. Oil on canvas
60x80 cm
Paris
Musée d'Orsay

Still life with open drawer
1877/1879. Oil on canvas
33x47 cm
Private Collection

Still life,
Pears and green Apples
1873/1877. Oil on canvas
22x32 cm
Paris
Musée de l'Orangerie

Green Apples
1873. Oil on canvas
26x32 cm
Paris
Musée d'Orsay

For lack of money, Cézanne did not take part in the second Impressionist exhibition, in 1876. He was too discouraged by the previous experiences to risk being a target for the critics yet again and without much hope of selling more than one picture. Furthermore, having been turned down by the Salon once more, he preferred to miss attending it and go down to Provence in spring. Life had taught him not to get too upset about the failure of his work to be understood: "I can perfectly understand that it couldn't be accepted, because of my initial standpoint, which is too far away from the target, that's to say representing nature." Every time he went to l'Estaque, Cézanne was always overwhelmed at rediscovering the light of Provençal landscapes, and became increasingly attracted to the sharpness and contrasts they contained. Whereas the delicate sky of Ile-de-France lent itself to the process of breaking up the subject with small analytical brushstrokes, l'Estaque offered him a synthetic vision. Forms were no longer dissolved in light or transposed in a hazy, unclear atmosphere. Cézanne had learned that instead of the diffuse light dear to the Impressionists, what he needed was bright, dazzling light, and that the dry atmosphere and sharply delineated shapes of the natural environment were exactly right for the way he wanted to paint. When he painted *Landscape with Red Roof* (*Pinetree in l'Estaque*), it was six years since Cézanne had last set foot

in the little fishing village nestling in a bay, and when we compare this work with others painted at the time of the war, we can see that there has been a striking development. Not only has the artist benefited from Pissarro's teaching in using a palette of brighter colors, but it is in this landscape with its dazzling summer sunshine that Cézanne has found the essential and intangible structures of the natural world. From now on the whole canvas has a firm structure, if only through color: the red of a roof, the white of walls, the green of vegetation and the blue of the sea. No precise source of light can now be pinpointed, because it is replaced by the strength of the colors themselves. It is this strength of color that defines objects existentially and distances them from the spectator.

In the third Impressionist exhibition, in May 1877, Cézanne once again yielded to the temptation of taking part. He exhibited seventeen paintings and was attacked by the press just as savagely as the previous time. Zola likewise just as carefully refrained from defending his friend. He came to the exhibition merely to take notes, which he used for his novel *L'Œuvre (the Masterpiece)*, the hero of which was closely based on Cézanne. Fortunately, amid this climate of fierce antagonism an occasional sane voice was heard to speak up: "The artist who has been most attacked and mistreated by the press and the public for the last fifteen years is Mr. Cézanne. Every scandalous epithet has been hurled at him, and his work has always been the object of mirth and it continues. Personally, I do not know of any painting that deserves to be laughed at less than this." Thus did Georges Rivière, an art critic and friend of Renoir, speak out on behalf of Cézanne. He continues: "Mr. Cézanne as an artist is like a Greek of the classi-

Folding Palette belonging to Paul Cézanne
Paris
Musée d'Orsay

Bouquet with Yellow Dahlia ●
1873. Oil on canvas
54x64 cm
Paris
Musée d'Orsay

Dahlias
1873. Oil on canvas
73x54 cm
Paris
Musée d'Orsay

cal period. His canvases exude the calmness and heroic serenity of ancient terra-cotta ceramics and decoration [...] His still lifes are so beautiful and so precise in the harmony of their tones, and there is a sort of solemn truth about them. This artist moves us in all of his pictures, because he himself experiences such powerful emotion at the sight of nature and has the skill and knowledge to capture it on canvas." Rivière was in fact one of the few contemporaries of Cézanne to understand this new pictorial language imbued with sensations. Among the still lifes referred to by Rivière are the *Still Life with Open Drawer* and *Still Life with Soup Tureen*, which demonstrate such mastery of composition and color. There is a skillful interplay between the curves and volumes (apple, bottle and tureen) on the one hand and the straight lines and flat surfaces on the other (pictures, wall and table), producing a particularly harmonious canvas. The first still lifes were influenced by the modern and classical French masters of the genre such as Chardin, as in *Cézanne's Accessories, Still Life with Medallion of Philippe Solari* and, like them, Cézanne selected familiar, simple objects that turned up again in other canvases. This economy of means applied to the choice of fruit, chosen by the artist for their shape and color, as well as for their freshness for practical reasons (*Green Apples*, and *Still Life with Pears*

Flowers in a blue vase
1880. Oil on canvas
30x23 cm
Paris
Musée de l'Orangerie

Flowers and Fruits
1879/1882. Oil on canvas
35x21 cm
Paris
Musée de l'Orangerie

**Madame Cézanne in a Striped Skirt /
or Madame Cézanne in a Red Armchair**
1877. Oil on canvas
72,5x56 cm
Boston
Museum of Fine Arts

and Green Apples). It is well known how much time Cézanne took over every canvas (Vollard commented: "If you had never seen Cézanne paint, you couldn't imagine how slow and laborious he was some days"), and that is perhaps why Provençal fruits such as figs and grapes, that were too likely to rot, are never found in his pictures and for the same reason there are not many flowers in his still lifes. Nevertheless there are a few superb exceptions, *Bouquet with Yellow Dahlia*, and *Dahlias*.

A picture painted at this time, the portrait of *Madame Cézanne in a Striped Skirt*, is one of some forty portraits that Cézanne made of his wife. Although she never shared her husband's passion for painting or for cultural life in general, she had exemplary patience and over the years she posed for him for countless hours. She preferred the elegance of Parisian life to their uneventful existence in Provence. But it has to be said that the first years of their life together gave her good reason to dislike the region that Cézanne was so fond of. For eight years he felt obliged to hide the relationship from his father lest he cancel his monthly allowance, and it was only in 1886 that the relationship was "legalised". This was a somewhat farcical paradox when it is remembered that Cézanne's parents themselves did not marry until five years after their son was born. As in this case, most of the portraits of Hortense depict her with severe features and an impenetrable and harsh expression on her face. And yet in this picture, she displays a certain coquetry about her appearance that is not found in any of the others. Hortense is wearing a handsome striped skirt and a jacket elegantly fastened with a big bow. Likewise, she has her hair up in a chignon, which is a change from the austere hairstyle with a central parting seen in so many of the other portraits. A casual observer might assume, wrongly, that this painting reflects a happy and harmonious bourgeois marriage...

Maturity 3

Scene from the jas de Bouffan
1875/1876. Oil on canvas
44x59 cm
Private Collection

Farmyard in Auvers
1879/1880. Oil on canvas
65x54 cm
Paris
Musée d'Orsay

Between 1877 and 1882 Cézanne did not take part in any exhibitions, but some of his pictures were nevertheless to be seen in Père Tanguy's shop. This is where, prompted by admirers like Monet, art critics such as Roger Marx and Geffroy saw them and began to be interested in Cézanne's work. Despite this interest on the part of a handful of enlightened individuals, derisive articles were still the order of the day in the Paris newspapers, and Cézanne was unwilling to exhibit with the Impressionists any longer. Paradoxically, Cézanne still made desperate efforts to be accepted by the Salon, despite the fact that he and the Impressionists had been united against that institution in their common struggle for public recognition. Moreover, the artist had other grounds for concern. His existence was still poisoned by family conflict, and he divided his time between the South (*Scene from the Jas de Bouffan*) and the capital. In Paris, throughout the time he was perfecting his mature painting techniques, Cézanne lived a lonely life similar to when he first moved there. He spent his mornings in museums, where he made studies of the ancients and of French classical sculptors (Sketchbook: *Study of Man on Horseback*, *Crouching Venus*). These sessions were his only training resource, and constituted a kind of daily warming up for his afternoon work painting out of doors or in his studio. Sometimes, his stays in Paris were short and he would occasionally be seen at the Nouvelle-Athènes Café, but most of the time he was in the South. Life in Provence was nevertheless stressful for Cézanne, as he constantly had to hurry back and forth between L'Estaque and Aix, where he had set up Hortense and their son in an apartment. He was still under his father's thumb financially, and continued to keep his liaison with Hortense secret. The father discovered the existence of his grandson Paul only six years later, in 1878, thanks to a careless remark by Victor Choquet. The tyrant's immediate response was to reduce his son's allowance by half, and the latter was obliged to ask Zola for help and to move away from Provence till the storm blew over.

● The jas de Bouffan (north side)

La Montagne Sainte-Victoire
1887/1890. Oil on canvas
65x92 cm
Paris
Musée d'Orsay

From April 1879 to March 1880, he lived in Melun, southeast of Paris, and found himself particularly inspired by the lively rivers and the poplar trees in that area. *The Poplars* is further proof of his sensitivity to the delicate landscapes of Ile-de-France, which are so different from the dry, exposed natural settings near Aix. So we now find the same muted halftones of the Auvers landscapes, with the difference that Cézanne's technique has now changed a lot and he is beginning to develop the inimitable style of his mature period. Furthermore his sense of composition has become more dynamic, despite the fact that the verticals of the tree trunks and the unclear mass of foliage that make up the landscape would naturally seem more difficult to structure. The right-hand third of the picture has been filled with a network of such freely executed vertical lines that one is almost entitled to consider it a "premonition" of abstract art. The other two thirds, on the other hand, conform to a more traditional compositional plan, due to the long diagonal line formed by the tops of the trees. The horizontal line of the crest of hills in the distance, which is partly obscured by the curtain of trees, separates the composition into two sections, while the light and geometric mass of the wall on the right is counterbalanced by the equally light but sinuous path winding off into the distance to the left. *The Bridge at Maincy, near Melun* goes well beyond impressionism by virtue of the density of its composition, and is one of Cézanne's most famous landscapes. By comparison with what one could expect in a Corot, there is no anecdotal or sentimental dimension to this composition. Feeling is now generated only by the

Study of man on horseback
1895. Pencil
15x23 cm
Paris
Louvre, D.A.G. (fonds Orsay)

Crouching Venus
1895. Pencil
15x23 cm
Paris
Louvre, D.A.G. (fonds Orsay)

effects of light and shade on the subject treated and by the relationship between shapes and colors. In this respect it may be argued that the subject gains in "dignity" since in order to be justified as a chosen topic, the landscape does not have to be supported by one of those intrusive but usually banal items. Cézanne will never feel the need to put a shepherdess or a cow in the middle of his marvelous landscapes to legitimize his choice of subject. Nor does he use the small brushstrokes that he employed in his Impressionist period, but instead skillfully builds up patches of color. This treatment is in fact the culmination of Cézanne's self-distancing from impressionism, which constantly sought to dissolve forms. The patches of color create harmonies with each other, finally becoming simple geometric shapes and acquiring a unity that has almost the symmetry and density of a crystal structure. Cézanne, in contrast to Gauguin (who was soon to buy two of his pictures from Tanguy, only for Cézanne to criticize him scornfully in public), did not use large monochrome surfaces but "constructed" the subject by means of colored patches of paint. The rectangular brushstrokes are laid on obliquely rather in the way bricks eventually

The green Jug
1885/1887. Pencil and watercolor
on white paper
22x24 cm
Paris
Louvre, D.A.G. (fonds Orsay)

Portrait of the Artist's Son
c. 1883/1885. Oil on canvas
35x38 cm
Paris
Musée de l'Orangerie

make up a whole wall. The association of water and trees is a recurrent theme in Cézanne's work and the way in which the structure of the bridge is at one with the vegetation, made up of the slanting branches of the trees, creates a perfectly unified structure. It results in a very precise network of geometrical lines dividing up the surfaces of the vegetation and the water. As with *The Poplars*, the restricted range of colors in Cézanne's palette is striking, which not only reflects the real tones of the scene depicted but also has the effect of enhancing the power of the composition.

In 1880, Cézanne visited Zola, whose novel *L'Assommoir* and the play based on it had brought him great wealth and fame. But Zola had changed a lot, and in Cézanne's uncompromising eyes, he had become a ceremonious bourgeois like so many others. Nevertheless Cézanne accepted the great writer's invitation to stay at his sumptuous house at Médan. This was situated on the Seine, west of

The Poplars
1879/1882. Oil on canvas
65x81 cm
Paris
Musée d'Orsay

Paris, and Cézanne enjoyed painting in the region, but perhaps without Zola realizing it, the spark had gone out of their friendship and Cézanne did not prolong the stay. Much more than the fact of having changed his life-style, Cézanne doubtless felt a grudge against Zola for never really having believed in his talent, and it must be said that the writer's assessments of the artist were not always glowing: "Paul may have the genius of a great painter, but he will never have the genius to become one. The slightest setback plunges him into despair." In other circumstances Zola had written: "Monsieur Paul Cézanne, possessing the temperament of a great painter still struggling to perfect his technique, remains nearer to Courbet and Delacroix". Only the juvenilia justify a comparison with Courbet and Delacroix, yet Zola formulated this appraisal at a time when Cézanne had already gone through his Impressionist phase. The writer was thus putting his literary talent at the service of artistic myopia. In truth, if the latter ever supported Cézanne, it was only financially and never through a real understanding of his art. Furthermore the Zola couple had never really been understanding about the liaison with Hortense. They jokingly referred to her as *La Boule* (ball or bowl), perhaps because of the shape of her head, giving a lead to others who tried to go one better by calling her son *Le Boulet* (millstone or cannonball). Leaving behind all this malice and stupidity, the *Portrait of the Artist's Son* depicts Paul junior at the age of about nine. This is the first really complete portrait of the boy in oils, whereas there are a number of drawings of him dating from earlier years. Clearly the interminable sittings that Cézanne always required must have been very testing for the lad. The back of the chair that we see in this fine, attractive painting is the same as the one in *Portrait of Madame Cézanne in a Striped Skirt*. Putting this shape behind the child's head is characteristic of the artist (as we see with an object as banal as *The Green Jug*): Cézanne thus wishes every subject to be echoed by a clear outer structure. This close-up compositional basis helps to focus on the subject, without any extraneous distraction. Mention must also be made of the fine chromatic values, in which the large dark masses and their smooth Indian ink finish enhance the bluish monochrome against which the flesh tints and two red touches of the lips and cheek are finely highlighted. This work is both simple and yet remarkably assured and in its strength and timelessness it reminds us strikingly of Gauguin – and once again we can only be puzzled by Cézanne's lifelong indifference to Gauguin's art. Throughout his life, Cézanne worshipped his son who looked after him in his old age and became his sole heir.

At the beginning of the 1880s, Cézanne was in a restless mood, largely because of the family ties that did not really leave him enough time to work in peace. Failure seemed to greet him at every turn. He was always up against a father who treated him with scorn and suspicion, his elder sister was gradually getting

The Bridge at Maincy
1879. Oil on canvas
58x72 cm
Paris
Musée d'Orsay

the upper hand and his wife did not understand the first thing about his painting. In addition to which, things were no better outside his family. Social relationships, to which Zola attached so much importance, were wretchedly beyond the comprehension of Cézanne. The more he felt excluded, the more he shunned contacts. This was without doubt why he found unfailing solace in nature, where he sought to discern the underlying structure of every object. After an unhappy stay at Zola's house, Cézanne found asylum with Pissarro in Pontoise in 1881, then with Renoir in La Roche-Guyon. He then went to Marseille, where he met the painter Monticelli. He was tired by all these wanderings and spent May to December 1883 in Aix. From there, he went to Gardanne and then L'Estaque, where he rented a little house with a garden near the station, and painted a new series of pictures. We have already seen how often Cézanne painted the picturesque village with its factory chimneys and rooftops. Further down there were jagged rocks and then the wide bay with its changing moods at the whim of the mistral wind at the foot of rows of houses on the slopes of the village: all of this made L'Estaque a constant source of subjects for the artist. Increasingly, since painting *The Bridge at Maincy near Melun*, Cézanne's work was developing a stronger pictorial structure, with color acquiring an importance of its own. Henceforth there was to be no break in the atmospheric unity created by brushwork and the simplification of volumes, no introduced "anecdotal" subject such as people or animals, etc. And in fact that is what we realize when we see these views of L'Estaque where no extraneous object or person is introduced into the picture just to create an effect. Indeed, Cézanne often climbed to the top of the neighboring hills to get the best perspective on the landscape, and this enabled him not only to handle the forms in a synthetic way but also to avoid the temptation of trivial, incidental details. With the magnificent landscape *L'Estaque seen from the Gulf of Marseille*, we may fully appreciate just how acute an observer of nature Cézanne had become. Yet being faithful to nature did not mean superficially reproducing what he saw. Far from being just an imitator, a copyist, Cézanne remained faithful to reality above all through the relationships between colors and forms in space. It was a question of translating into the language of painting a new harmony that he himself called "the parallel harmony to nature". In the end it was all a matter of equivalence. In this picture, the tension inherent in the diagonal of the hill contrasts with the tranquillity of the grandiose landscape, just as the blue of the sea seems intensified by the orange tones in the foreground. Curiously in fact, despite the luminous power of this work, Cézanne's palette range is quite limited, but then within this range he modulates his tones quite considerably. Light falls with equal intensity over the whole of the canvas. Colors and forms seem to be complementary in their effects, breaking down reality into a magnificent set of colorful building blocks.

The Sea at l'Estaque
1883/1886. Oil on canvas
73x92 cm
Paris
Musée Picasso

**The Gulf of Marseille
seen from l'Estaque**
1886/1890. Oil on canvas
76x97 cm
Chicago
The Art Institute of Chicago

According to Cézanne, the surface of a picture had to have a uniform structure, and vulgar "copying" of reality by unnecessary illusionist effects must be avoided. Forms and colors have the same importance in this vision and had to be equally perceptible in every part of the composition. In the absence of a concrete presence, which pertains to the "real" world, what objects are denoted by is thus color, and the different areas of a picture are differentiated evenly, with the result that the whole work acquires a crystal clear sharpness. During this mature and fruitful period of his career, with impressionism left well behind him and replaced by his own distinctive touch on canvas, Cézanne took more and more pleasure in painting the same subjects. As he never ceased to observe and experiment, his technique became increasingly rigorous. *The Sea at L'Estaque*, which was acquired by Picasso in the 1940s, also betokens a new desire by the artist to confer solidity in the picture. Here he uses a rather classic compositional layout, namely horizontals (literally a horizon, and the line of the road) crossed by the verticals of the two trees in the foreground and the chimney. This way of creating an impression of depth harks back to the baroque tradition of the *repoussoir*, (whereby a foreground or lateral device leads the eye further in). It is a major factor in the success of this particularly fluent work, with such a calm expanse of water in the background contrasting with the trees, handled with the suppleness of pen and ink, and the village, which nestles in picturesque manner on the slope of the hill. The eye follows the path, which crosses the picture in the foreground then goes down the hill towards the village and finishes at the water. The light, far from blanketing the different elements of the picture evenly in impressionist manner, is clearly conveyed by brushstrokes. Another picture using the same setting, *The Gulf of Marseille seen from L'Estaque*, of which Cézanne made several versions, was one of the first works by the artist to be acquired by a French museum, in 1894, thanks to the Caillebotte bequest. Until 1890 Cézanne continued to paint this exact view, with L'Estaque and its factory chimneys in the foreground. This is a unique setting, if ever there was one, a landscape subtly combining as its main elements the motionless background expanse of water with the neat cubes of the houses and the irregular patches of trees and foliage. This beautiful spot also inspired Zola, who had this to say about it in his short story *Naïs Micoulin*: "The country is superb. On each side of the Gulf, a rocky spur stretches out into the sea, while islands seem to block off the horizon in the distance; and the sea is just like a vast lake of intense blue when the weather is fine. [...] The coastline sets off from Marseille, curves round and breaks up into wide indentations as it reaches L'Estaque, where now and then the lines of factories send tall plumes of smoke into the sky. When the sun is high overhead, the sea becomes almost black and appears to be sleeping in between the two rocky promontories whose

L'Estaque,
view of the Gulf of Marseille
1878/1880. Oil on canvas
59,5x73 cm
Paris
Musée d'Orsay

whiteness is mottled with yellow and brown in the heat. The pines are like a dark green stain on the surrounding reddish earth. It is a huge picture, a glimpse of the Orient, vanishing in the shimmering, blinding daylight." Later Cézanne abandoned the "huge picture" that was L'Estaque because of the gradual encroachment of industry, and today this beautiful place has been invaded by factories and Marseille port installations. Cézanne felt the loss deeply, and wrote about it to his niece in 1902: "I have a very clear memory of the coast at L'Estaque, which used to be so picturesque. Unfortunately, what people call progress is nothing but the invasion of bipeds, who are never happy until they have turned everything into hideous docks with gas lamps and, worse, electric lighting. What an age we live in!" Painted before progress ruined the tranquillity so beloved by Cézanne, the composition of *Gulf of Marseille seen from L'Estaque* is divided into three clearly defined parts: first the landscape of hills, then the sea, and finally the mountains and the coastline with the sky completing the picture in the background. In this work, with its skillfully created atmosphere, instead of just using the aerial perspective of the Impressionists, which would have meant creating the effect of distance by attenuating and blurring colors in the background, Cézanne retains the same sharpness of color for the three successive grounds. Far from using the artifice as the Impressionists would, he creates the effect of depth mainly by omitting detail in the background and by the strict arrangement of the architectural motifs in the foreground. Once again, light emanates uniformly from the very interior of the objects making up the picture, and Cézanne provides no shadow that might point to the source of this light. Cézanne's misanthropy was increasingly pronounced, and his happiness was derived from long sessions on his own, working in the open air. Moreover, this did not mean that he was forgotten by his fellow painters. In 1884, Renoir went down to the Côte d'Azur in quest of new subjects and met Cézanne in Marseille. Impressionism was then going through a crisis from which it was destined never to recover, and many artists were beginning to leave the movement in search of new directions (in fact 1884 was the year when the Salon of Independent Artists came into being). During his stay, Renoir caught pneumonia and Cézanne's mother took him in and nursed him. Despite the state of his health, Renoir went with Cézanne to paint the Mont Sainte-Victoire. The result is very instructive: whereas Renoir's version is evanescent, for Cézanne the subject is above all firmly structured, in the overall composition as much as in the detail. No comparison could be more conclusive in demonstrating the difference between an impressionist's perception and Cézanne's. This is perhaps why the next generation of young painters, feeling that all the life had gone out of Impressionism, began to feel increasingly curious about the master painter of Aix.

Five Female Bathers
1877/1878. Oil on canvas
45x55 cm
Paris
Musée Picasso

However, in the quest for the underlying structure of the physical world, landscape was not the only area of exploration for a pictorial solution. The human body was also a wide subject for artistic experiment, and the most important of Cézanne's themes was undoubtedly that of male and female bathers. He was so obsessed with it that it has been estimated that he devoted nearly one hundred and fifty paintings, watercolors and drawings to it. This amazing production is spread over the whole of his career, and the seeds of it were already present in certain works of his youth, where numerous natural décors were the setting for confrontation between love and death, elegy and "Panic" frenzy. After the 1870s, this theme or genre was gradually exploited more calmly as Cézanne gained greater control over his own passions. In fact an attempt to portray harmony between human beings in a natural setting can be found in certain pastoral scenes of his youth in which bathers were increasingly prominent. This general theme, derived from Cézanne's own personal memories, particularly his excursions as a boy to swim in the river Arc with Zola, slowly expanded to become a substantial artistic genre. This is what we see in *Five Female Bathers*, in which sitting and standing figures alternate and the bodies are really studies of rhythmic variations, but some of the tension of Cézanne's youthful handling of this theme is still perceptible. Gradually, as he matured, Cézanne separated male from female bathers, who in the past had been locked in violent conflict, and the expressive and erotic bodies of the orgiastic scenes were slowly replaced by bodies that were almost devoid of sexuality. What is surprising in a work like *Three Female Bathers*, on the other hand, is the undeniable clumsiness of the anatomical depiction, notably as regards the woman sitting on the left. In fact, for his models Cézanne very often used classical painting and ancient sculpture (Sketch Album: After *the Borghese Ares*, *Satyr with Cymbals*, but he did so mainly for compositional purposes rather than for capturing accurate expressions or movements. At the end of his life Cézanne spoke about his difficulties in this area to Émile Bernard who was, with Gauguin, one of the originators of *Cloisonniste* painting and Synthetism: "As you know, I have often made sketches of male and female bathers that I would have preferred to make bigger and from life: the lack of a model means I have had to limit myself to these rough sketches. There were all sorts of difficulties such as finding a setting that might not be too different from what I had in mind, like getting several people together at the same time, getting men and women to pose nude in exactly the positions I wished. And finally, there was also the problem of transporting a large canvas, the thousand and one difficulties of getting the right weather, setting everything up and the mass of equipment required for a work of considerable size. So I had to postpone my project for a complete new version of a Poussin from life not constructed from notes, drawings and bits of studies. In other words, what I

Bathers
1892/1894. Oil on canvas
22x33 cm
Paris
Musée d'Orsay

would like is a real, open-air Poussin, full of color and light, instead of one of those works thought out in the studio, in which everything has a murky color resulting from poor daylight and the absence of reflections from the sky and natural light." Cézanne was in fact pathologically shy in the presence of nude models and to capture the human form, he had to resort to photographs and his old studies from the Académie Suisse. Hence, his clumsiness in depicting nudes can perhaps be explained as much by his personal inhibitions as by any desire to incorporate the human body into his vast enterprise of "deconstructing" the subject.

For a short while, in 1885, Cézanne was enmeshed in a perplexing love relationship, the only one he ever experienced apart from his brief love for Hortense. But his desires were unfulfilled, and he chose to take refuge from the tyranny of emotion by going to stay with Renoir in La Roche-Guyon. After four weeks, he went on to Vernon. It is a pity that so little is known about this late-season passion, which took this normally misogynistic man by surprise at the age of forty-five, but the die was cast as far as his love life was concerned. With the exception of his mother and his adored sister Marie, Cézanne scarcely had any female company in his life other than Hortense, virtually the only woman who modeled for him, before finally tiring of it. We see her in 1880 in *Madame Cézanne in the Garden*, with a vague, melancholy expression on her face. The impression of distance, which tends to keep all affective elements out of his painting, certainly reflects Cézanne's own problems in coping with the emotional conflicts in his life. And yet we must also attribute this to what he was striving for in his art: the quest for permanence, whether of people or of things. He set about painting portraits exactly as he did landscapes. It was through formal rigor that he conferred stature and permanence upon them. The fact that the setting in which the model poses is roughly sketched in oils creates an even greater sense of presence for the sitter. Motionless and monolithic in her black dress, Madame Cézanne has something of an ancient idol about her. Seeing this picture, one cannot help feeling the influence that Cézanne may have had on Picasso, obviously not only, during the Spaniard's "classic" period, but at many other times too.

In 1886 Cézanne went to stay with Choquet in Hattenville to paint, but this year saw also the publication of Zola's novel *The Masterpiece*, which came as a shock for the artist. Even if the link was clear only in the first part of the novel, Cézanne nevertheless recognized himself in the protagonist Claude Lantier, a failed painter who commits suicide, and this had the effect of putting a permanent end to the relationship between the two men who had been friends since childhood. Many of their mutual acquaintances must have felt as disturbed as Cézanne, as a good number of features of the novel were undeniably borrowed

The Bather
1885/1887. Oil on canvas
127x97 cm
New York
Museum of Modern Art

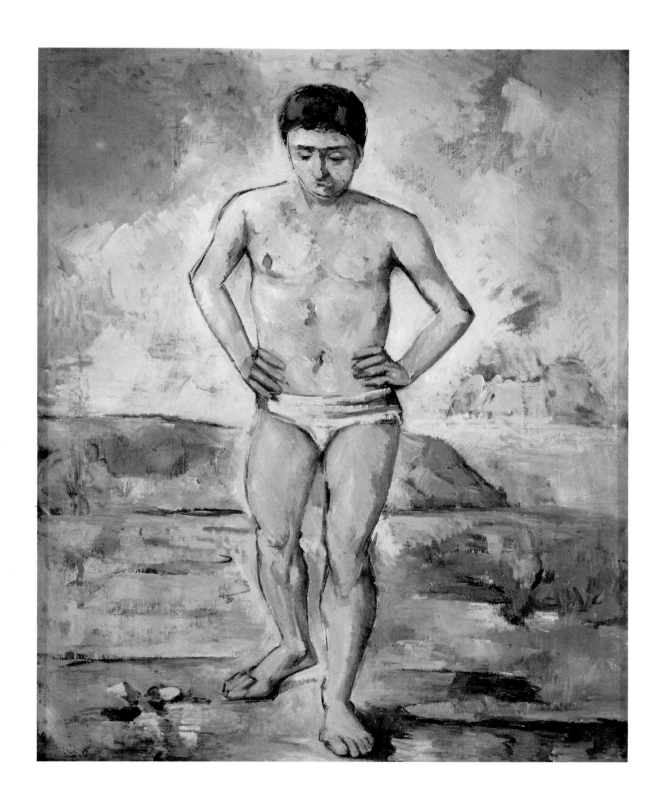

Three Females Bathers
1875/1877. Oil on canvas
22x19 cm
Paris
Musée d'Orsay

from reality, for example the allusion to the *Jas de Bouffan*, when Sandoz (Lantier's childhood friend) comes to visit: "The walls of the studio were in fact covered with a series of sketches done by the painter during a recent journey. It was as if they had the former horizons all around them, and the fierce blue sky above the reddish-brown countryside. In one, a plain stretches off into the distance, dotted about with small, gray olivetrees, and ends with the pinkish outlines of distant hills. In another, between scorched, rust-colored slopes, the bare trickle of water in the Viorne (i.e. the Arc) has almost dried up completely under the arch of an old bridge covered with white dust, the only vegetation being bushes killed by the drought. Further away, there was the Infernets Gorges, a gaping chasm full of fallen boulders, piled up chaotically, like a wild desert with waves of rock stretching to infinity. And there were all sorts of well known places: [...]; the Jas de Bouffan, as white as a mosque, set in its huge grounds resembling pools of blood; as well as many others." This was now the

Nude Man
1895. Pencil
13,3x21,7 cm
Paris
Louvre, D.A.G. (fonds Orsay)

Satyr with Cymbals
1895. Pencil
15x23 cm
Paris
Louvre, D.A.G. (fonds Orsay)

end of friendship for these two great men, who, at a very different time, had been children wandering around without a care in the beautiful Aix countryside. In April of the same year, when he returned from Gardanne, Cézanne at last married Hortense in Aix-en-Provence in the presence of his parents. The only reason after such a long time for legalizing a relationship with a woman whom he had long since ceased to love was doubtless the wish to put an end to the illegitimate status of his adored son Paul. Six months later, leaving his affairs in perfect order, Cézanne's father died at the age of eighty-eight, and the artist was able at last to get his hands on his inheritance. For the first time in his life, at forty-seven, he was independent. His financial situation was completely transformed. He inherited 400,000 francs a year, not counting the 25,000 francs left to Hortense and her son. Unfortunately there was a cloud on the horizon in that Cézanne would eventually have to part with his beloved *Jas de Bouffan* a few years after the death of his father because of his sisters' entitlements under the terms of the will, and he suffered greatly as a consequence. He always missed the great house, the farm the drive with its chestnut trees, the ornamental pond with its stone lions and dolphin, and above all the garden with its seasonal rhythms, from which the Mont Sainte-Victoire could be discerned in the distance behind large groves of sweet chestnut. Like Giverny for Monet, more than any other place, the Jas de Bouffan remains associated with Cézanne's work, although the artist's link with it is different. It is not a place that he selected and bought, but a family space that he knew before his career as a painter began, and in fact, strange though it may seem, it was not until 1885 that a picture was inspired by it, namely *House and Farm at Jas de Bouffan*. Depicting the house leaning to the left, this picture recreates an astonishing record of the parental home. Rigorously geometric in itself, in contrast with the jumbled shapes of the farm buildings, the house appears to be tilted. On the side facing the sun, the farm buildings actually mirror this strange lean to the left. This work was executed during the crucial period when Cézanne finally abandoned the Impressionists' techniques of fragmenting the image and substituted his constructivist discipline on landscapes whose architecture was conducive to his brand of structured vision (*Trees and Houses*). In this Prague version, the artist employs an unusually simple and direct palette (red, green and black); through its complementary colors this canvas offers a striking chromatic contrast, with the dark green of the grassy bank serving as a counterpoint to the red of the roof. The firm network of parallel and perpendicular lines ordering the composition already suggests in its discipline the layout of a cubist canvas.

Some time before having to give up the Jas de Bouffan, Cézanne sought new subjects and rented a small room looking out on the courtyard of the Château-Noir, a large property on an imposing site on the Tholonet road. He also rented a hut in the Bibémus Quarry, where he stored his equipment when he was working in the area. Once he could no longer paint his cherished family home, he consoled himself with a familiar motif that, although not as cherished as it ought to have been, at least was always there, his wife. Despite the fact that they were now legally married, Paul and Hortense Cézanne were strangers to one another.

Madame Cézanne in the garden
1879/1882. Oil on canvas
80x63 cm
Paris
Musée de l'Orangerie

While he dedicated himself exclusively to his art, Hortense spent most of her time in Paris with Paul, where she could enjoy the spectacle of high class luxurious life-styles. At various times of life, Cézanne had favorite models whom he painted over and over again. As we have seen, when he was young he made the most of his uncle Dominique. Then came Choquet, followed by some of the peasants at Bouffan, particularly, as we shall see, those who posed for the *Cardplayers* series. Yet until about 1890, it was Hortense that he depicted time and time again, two examples being the *Portrait of Madame Cézanne* in the Musée Granet and in the Musée d'Orsay, both dating from around 1885-1887. These portraits reflect in their way the same structured arrangement as the landscapes. In the Orsay portrait, which once belonged to Matisse, the sitter poses with statuesque motionlessness. The formal austerity of the composition, created through color and concentration on essentials, produces an unusual feeling of distance between the spectator and the model with her solemn and unyielding face. The impassive gaze "disincarnates" the sitter without however stripping her of the appearance of being alive. We should note the careful vertical separation of the background, juxtaposing two subdued tones yet creating a warm-color/cool-color contrast. This shock has a dynamic effect making the silhouette stand out with clarity and force. To get away from the unending lamentations of Hortense, Cézanne left the house every morning for Gardanne, a small mountain village in upper Provence. There, he painted several canvases that show via their composition amongst other things, that he now possessed a degree of confidence about himself as an artist. In these calm landscapes, Cézanne felt less and less in need of the approval of his fellows. His meticulous observation was what he was content to rely on. After some time, he rented a small house for himself and his family, in order not to have to travel the twenty kilometers every day that separated Gardanne from Aix. He had a view of Mont Sainte-Victoire (the south slope with arid foothills), to which subject he now wished to devote himself almost exclusively. As early as 1870, this same subject was an essential part of his picture *The Railway Cutting*. Like a bastion, an indestructible work of nature, Mont Sainte-Victoire began to be prominent among

Apotheosis of Delacroix •
1894. Oil on canvas
27x35 cm
Aix-en-Provence
Musée Granet

Cézanne's masterpieces, in time occupying the central place. This was the subject that he chose in his last years to capture the strength and permanence of the natural world, indeed to try to achieve a total fusion of all the elements within it. By devoting himself to this imposing view, Cézanne drew on a fresh source of hope that gave him the strength to go on working, despite the incomprehension of others. *La Montagne Sainte-Victoire with the Tall Pine*, with its delicate pale blue color range, is a symbol of both stability and permanence. From the practical point of view, we may also note, this is a landscape that suited Cézanne perfectly, given the length of time he took to handle a subject. Since he observed nature above all to detect what was intrinsic and eternal, variations in the atmosphere were of little consequence to him. In his view, the act of painting had two phases, and the actual depiction in the strict sense was always preceded by a difficult and arduous process of observation. As he himself put it, "You have to reflect. The eye is not enough. Reflection is vital." First he "decoded" or "deciphered" the subject, trying to identify its internal structure, then he planned the composition on the basis of the colors and forms that he had observed in the minutest detail, not "imagined" or simply "interpreted". After this long process of alchemy, the result could not be other than faithful to reality. The Courtauld *Sainte-Victoire* is a remarkably powerful work, and yet there is also something very gentle about it at the same time; it is the product of a refined sensibility working in perfect harmony with a rigorous and demanding intelligence. As in watercolor painting, certain areas of the canvas are left white, untouched by the brush. The branches of the tall pine espouse the curving outline of the mountain, and with its extreme simplification, for example turning the plain into a sort of chess board with alternating squares of green and ochre, the *Sainte-Victoire* is a counterpart to the famous *Hundred Views of Mount Fuji* painted in homage to the sacred mountain by the Japanese master Hokusai. We should remember that Cézanne was just one of a number of French artists who marveled at this series of woodcuts when they were published in 1883.

**House and farm
at jas de Bouffan**

1885/1887. Oil on canvas
60x73 cm
Prague
National Gallery

**The Plaster Kiln, also called the Mill
at the Trois Sautets Bridge**
1890/1894. Pencil and watercolor
42x53 cm
Paris
Louvre, D.A.G. (fonds Orsay)

Trees and Houses
1885/1888. Oil on canvas
54x73 cm
Paris
Musée de l'Orangerie

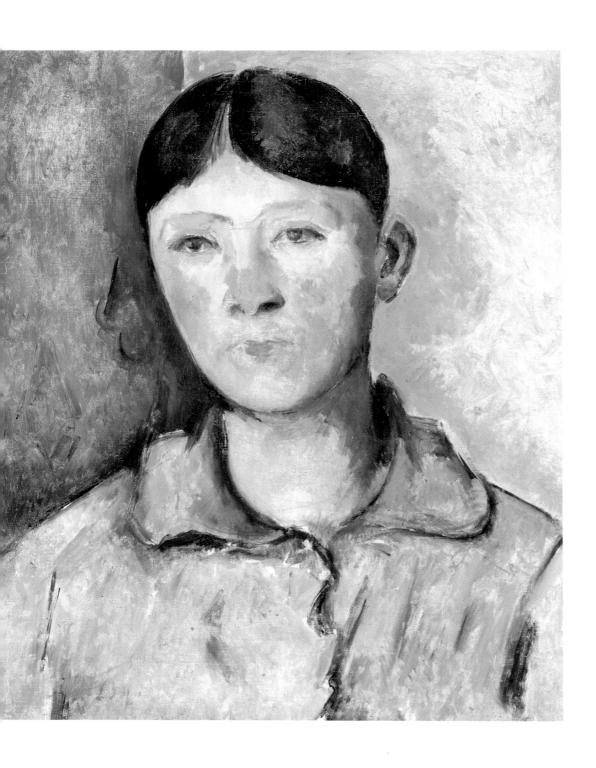

Portait of Madame Cézanne
1885/1887. Oil on canvas
47x39 cm
Paris
Musée d'Orsay

Portait of Madame Cézanne
1885/1887. Oil on canvas
46x38 cm
Aix-en-Provence
Musée Granet

La Montagne Sainte-Victoire with the Tall Pine

1885/1887. Oil on canvas
66x90 cm
London
Courtauld Institute

For Cézanne the intense light of the Midi made things appear as if they were located on the same plane, which, on the other hand, had the effect of making them more sharply delineated, and this depiction of the Mont Sainte-Victoire has the coherence and solidity of a crystal structure. Using the contrast between the color of the earth and of the vegetation, Cézanne in fact endeavored not only to capture the effects of light but also, more subtly, to relate pictorial surface to color values denoting space.

Cézanne's devotion to this mountain motif reflects his great love of nature and the consolation he could find in it. However, at about the time this picture was painted, Cézanne was still making hesitant efforts to appeal to the public. In the end, he succeeded in getting through the doors of the Salon only once. This was when one of his painter friends took advantage of a new regulation to pass off a painting by Cézanne as the work of one of his pupils, thus getting it accepted without being scrutinized by the selection committee. Unfortunately, this regulation was promptly scrapped and he wrote to his mother in the following terms: "I am beginning to believe myself better than those around me, and you know that the good opinion I have of my work has not come about casually. I still have to work hard, not to achieve a good finish, which is an aspect that dazzles idiots. That aspect, which is so commonly appreciated, is really a matter for craft trades and makes work inartistic and ordinary. I only have to try to complete things just to get closer to the truth and be more skillful. And you can be sure there comes a time when you are taken seriously, and then you have keener and more sincere admirers than those who are only flattered by a vain appearance."

Despite the general climate of misunderstanding, Cézanne agreed to take part in the 1887 Brussels exhibition at the invitation of Octave Mauss, secretary of an artistic group called the "The XX". This was a Belgian association set up in October 1883 that, despite its Impressionist and post-Impressionist leanings, organized an annual show for the whole of the European avant-garde. Although Cézanne had more or less given up hope of seeing any of his paintings on show in public, Choquet was still helpful and optimistic and managed to have The *House of the Hanged Man* exhibited at the 1889 World Fair, though it was so badly placed that neither the critics nor the public saw it. Despite the hostility towards him in the capital, Cézanne still lived in Paris for part of the year. In 1888, he rented a studio in rue Val-de-Grâce, where he painted *Pierrot and Harlequin* or *Mardi Gras*, for which the models were his son Paul (*Study for the "Mardi Gras" Harlequin*), and one of the son's friends, Louis Guillaume. During his boyhood in Aix, Cézanne had loved the annual Carnival, and this somewhat surprising subject can no doubt be put down to nostalgia for the carefree life of former times. Generally speaking, as the artist advanced in years he was subject to this mood more and more, and he in fact spoke of the pleasure he felt in

**Pierrot and Harlequin
or Mardi Gras**
1888/1889. Oil on canvas
102x81 cm
Moscow
Pushkin Museum

the company of young people through whom he could relive an existence that he had long since left behind. Be that as it may, this unusually light-hearted picture was prepared for by several drawings in the same vein, suggesting that it was not a one-off amusement but a pondered anticipation of a new subject that perhaps also evoked metaphorically the situation of the artist who is the butt of the public's derision and mirth. The work is also novel in another way. It is exceptional in that the sitters are not just juxtaposed but they relate to each other, as Pierrot seems to be trying to steal the stick from Harlequin, who is the focus. They are linked also in another way, this time fortuitously, by the complementary styles and colors of their costumes, which are given particularly careful treatment by the artist. Cézanne creates an impression of depth and space by applying the principle of warm colors (here the red) and cool colors (the blue): the red advances to the foreground, the blue recedes. While they may certainly be seen as theatre curtains, the ample wall hangings with their foliage design also anticipate the motifs that he was soon to make frequent use of in his fine still lifes, and that had already been given admirable treatment in watercolor (*The Curtains*).

Despite the apparent ordinariness of the theme, Cézanne executed this type of still life at all times of his career, and it was one of his favorite subjects. The range of themes in his still lifes was established as early as the beginning of the 1870s in some rather static compositions. It is still the case in *Apples and Biscuits*, a rather stiffly symmetrical composition with the fruit arranged in the middle of the canvas being apparently mirrored on each side of the vertical axis constituted precisely by the lock of the chest. The plate is the only thing to disrupt this orderly arrangement, not only in being an intrusion in itself but also in that the color of it picks up the warm tones of the fruit. In *Fruit, Cloth and Milk Can*, whereas the lock of the chest still marks the vertical axis of the canvas (which is further accentuated by the glass), the fruit is now skillfully arranged at random, and the wall as well as the white cloth with its ample folds are a foretaste of the still lifes of the 1890s. The *Still Life with Basket, or Kitchen Table* shows Cézanne moving towards a fairly characteristic radical transformation of the way in which the theme is treated spatially. In this composition the motifs have become more numerous, to the extent that now it is almost as appropriate to talk of a landscape as of a still life. The different objects are no longer isolated and separate from each other but rather they subtly and mysteriously interrelate according to their shapes and colors. Although space is clearly defined by the furniture, the perspective seems to be willfully distorted. In fact, once the accessories in the composition were carefully arranged, Cézanne constructed a pictorial space conforming to his own totally subjective laws but intended to assure a harmonious relationship between the different parts of the picture.

Study for the
Mardi Gras Harlequin ●
1888. Pencil on paper
24x30 cm
Paris
Louvre D.A.G. (fonds Orsay)

Still life with Basket,
or Kitchen Table
1881. Oil on canvas
65x81 cm
Paris
Musée d'Orsay

Roses in a Green Vase
1885/1895. Watercolor on pencil
23x31cm
Paris
Louvre, D.A.G. (fonds Orsay)

The Curtains
c. 1885. Gouache, pencil
and watercolor
49x30 cm
Paris
Louvre, D.A.G. (fonds Orsay)

Apples and Biscuits
c. 1880. Oil on canvas
45x55 cm
Paris
Musée de l'Orangerie

● The jas de Bouffan (south side)

Flowers Pots
1883/1887. Gouache, pencil
and watercolor
23x30 cm
Paris
Louvre, D.A.G. (fonds Orsay)

Still life
● **Fruits, Cloth and Milk Can**
1879/1882. Oil on canvas
60x73 cm
Paris
Musée de l'Orangerie

We see that although everything in the depiction is plausible, nothing is possible: neither the perspective, which appears disrupted from different angles, nor the arrangement of the objects, which are balanced very precariously. In fact this "simultaneous image" of objects with different perspectives and scales in one respect heralds cubism. For his still lifes, as well as for a number of his other favorite themes throughout his career, Cézanne often used watercolor, a medium that he handled with great skill and that brought a subtle counterpoint effect to his powerful compositions through its delicacy. There are a great number of them - more than four hundred have been identified to date – but before their exhibition organized by Ambroise Vollard in 1905, they were scarcely known about beyond a small circle of collectors such as Choquet, Pellerin and Count Camondo. In fact, at the end of his life, Cézanne bought from Vollard a watercolor of flowers by Delacroix, another great master of the genre. *Flowers Pots* is a magnificent example of these delicate watercolors with fine lines. Within the exquisite simplicity of the composition there is a sense of economy particularly appropriate for the subtle effects obtainable in this medium. The very graphic horizontal line of the wooden shelf and the sensitively aligned flowerpots give full expression to the exuberance of the draftsmanship and coloring of the vegetation. Cézanne began painting bouquets of flowers in the 1870s as a result of contact with the Impressionists. While the works executed in that decade depict bouquets just on their own, those of the 1880s mix flowers with fruit, as in *The Blue Vase*. This splendid, gracious composition retains the rhythm and sensitive touch of Cézanne's watercolors, and the two strident notes of the red flowers and the fruit harmonize miraculously with the delicately modulated blues of the vase.

The Blue Vase

1885/1887. Oil on canvas
61x50 cm
Paris
Musée d'Orsay

From recognition to posterity

Portrait of Gustave Geffroy

1895. Oil on canvas
116x89 cm
Paris
Musée d'Orsay

The years 1894-1895 were a decisive time for Cézanne, who had hardly appeared on the artistic scene for a quarter of a century. In March 1894, the art critic Théodore Duret put his collection on sale. It contained three pictures by Cézanne that fetched healthy prices, ranging between 600 and 800 francs. A few weeks later this sale was followed by that of Père Tanguy's collection, at which the dealer Ambroise Vollard bought six Cézannes. On the occasion of this sale, the author Geffroy published a brilliant article about him: "Cézanne has become a sort of precursor, a reference point for the Symbolists, and just from a factual point of view there is absolutely a definite link between his painting and that of Gauguin and Bernard, etc., and even the art of Van Gogh. For this only, Cézanne deserves to be recognized and respected. Another question worth examining is whether there is an essential spiritual link between Cézanne and his disciples, and whether Cézanne supports the same synthetist theories as the Symbolists. It is easy today to form an idea of the way in which Cézanne's art has developed overall. We can say with absolute certainty that in his attitude to nature, Cézanne bases himself on no artistic theory; he in no way tyrannizes nature or makes it conform to any preconceived law or artistic formula of any sort whatsoever. This does not mean that he has no program, law or ideal. These have not come to him from the world of art, but from the depths of his curiosity, from his desire to absorb into his own consciousness the things that he sees and admires." In that same month, March 1894, it became known that Gustave Caillebotte, who had died the previous year, had bequeathed his collection to the nation. Gustave Geffroy then published a list of the works making up Caillebotte's collection, with short paragraphs on the major paintings, including an enumeration and account of those works by Cézanne. The destiny of the greatest masterpieces is sometimes bewildering when one learns that, as he found the commission exhausting, Cézanne regretted having agreed to paint the *Portrait of Gustave Geffroy*, and in fact did not complete it. In the spring of 1895, in recognition of the praise he had received from him, Cézanne undertook to paint a portrait of Geffroy in his study, devoting almost daily sittings to the task from early April to mid June. He dined with the sitter and the latter's mother, and introduced wide-ranging criticism of every aspect of modern life into their conversations. Unfortunately, Cézanne then wrote the following letter to Geffroy in June: "Dear Monsieur Geffroy, being about to leave, and unable to complete the task, which I regret having undertaken, I beg you to excuse me and to hand the things I left in your library to the messenger I shall be sending round...". However, Geffroy managed to persuade Cézanne to give it one more week, and before setting off for Aix, Cézanne promised to finish the portrait on his return. Nevertheless, Cézanne changed his mind and sent a messenger to collect his equipment, although leaving the picture. Geffroy and Cézanne were never to meet again, and although the writer continued to collect and praise Cézanne's work in his articles, Cézanne had particularly harsh words for him in return. The reasons for this change of mind have never been explained, but Geffroy was a Liberal and defender of Dreyfus, whereas Cézanne had become more and more reactionary over the years. This development may seem surprising in a visionary, but we must remember that he was his father's son, and something of the latter's inflexible character had perhaps been inherited by him. Whatever the reason, with its remarkably delicate color range, the portrait of Geffroy is one of Cézanne's most famous portraits, doubtless in part because of the exceptional number of sittings involved, and one of his masterpieces in all genres. The power of the composition derives in large measure from the subtlety of its astonishing and complex construction. The equilibrium of the latter is produced by the harmonious way in which all the elements of the picture interrelate. Every object for Cézanne must have its place, and the resulting harmony could only be achieved after considerable reflection. Thus the artist took great care about the way in which the objects were arranged on the table, from the plaster Rodin statuette visible on the left to the paper flower that he brought with him especially (as natural flowers wither too quickly).

The Caillebotte Bequest had far greater consequences than just this brief acquaintanceship between Cézanne and Geffroy. There was a public outcry, and a great number of politicians, critics and influential academic painters voiced their protests. As executor of the will, Renoir had to make concessions to ensure that the collection went where it was meant to go, into the Musée du Luxembourg. Thus only two Cézannes were accepted, despite Renoir's best efforts. Yet again, Cézanne's art was confronted with almost unanimous hostility. When in the same year Cézanne went to Giverny to spend some time with Monet, the latter arranged an anniversary celebration to which were invited a small group of friends, including Geffroy, the novelist and critic Octave

Portrait of Ambroise Vollard ●
1899. Oil on canvas
100x81 cm
Paris
Petit Palais

Mirbeau, Rodin and Clemenceau. Appreciative gestures like this ought to have consoled Cézanne for the chronic neglect of which he was the victim, but the niceties of social life had always been a form of torture for him, and were to remain so. He had in fact long since given up mixing in polite society, where his friends had tried for such a long time in vain to invite him. Feeling always unappreciated despite the changing times, his prickly character did not mellow with age and he turned more and more in on himself. A little later Monet organized another lunch, this time specifically in Cézanne's honor, to which Renoir, Sisley and others were invited, but the painter was touchy and hostile. Nevertheless, in much more concrete terms, 1895 brought Cézanne something of the support and appreciation that he so needed. A young art dealer who had just set up in business, Ambroise Vollard, got in touch with Cézanne's son to organize what was to be the artist's first solo exhibition. It opened in November 1895 in a gallery in rue Laffitte. There was not enough room for the one hundred and fifty canvases that Cézanne had sent, so they had to be hung in batches in rotation. The Vollard exhibition was a big step forward for Cézanne's reputation. Four years later, the dealer asked Cézanne to paint his portrait (*Portrait of Ambroise Vollard*). Vollard had a somewhat fanciful character and the amusing account he gave of the sittings contains perhaps an element of exaggeration. They began at eight in the morning and lasted until eleven-thirty, and the breaks for the sitter could hardly be shorter, as Hortense had had good reason to know over the years. Cézanne's progress was painfully slow, but Vollard was extremely eager to have the portrait completed and so took care not to offend Cézanne. After no fewer than one hundred and fifteen sittings, Cézanne had to break off and leave for the South, saying to his sitter apparently without the slightest trace of irony: "I think the shirt is coming on quite well." The resulting portrait is incomplete, with the eyes blank, as in certain other portraits, but it is a work of impressive sobriety and with an astonishing presence. It is a dark canvas with a brown background, and Vollard's right hand, painted in quickly in a warm tone that is practically the only living feature, is to the fore with the effect of breaking the vertical line formed by the shirt and the head. In 1895, when Vollard was getting enthusiastic about his pictures, Cézanne was in Aix, living with his aging mother, whose health problems kept him in the Midi longer than planned. In any case, regardless of the fact that he would naturally stay in the South to take

Standing Female Nude
1890/1895. Watercolor on pencil
89x53 cm
Paris
Louvre, D.A.G. (fonds Orsay)

care of the mother of whom he was so fond, Cézanne distanced himself increasingly from Paris and the modern world. He was aging prematurely, and had quarreled with all of his friends there and finally his diabetes problem did not help him control his moods. More than ever, he had ceased to seek artistic inspiration in city life, unlike Degas and Toulouse-Lautrec at this time. Significantly, it was the building of a minerals plant in the Rio valley that caused him to give up going to L'Estaque to paint. He was just the opposite of the Impressionists with their fascination with modernity and if he ever painted factory chimneys, it was only to use them objectively as elements in a landscape. He wanted to abolish time in a society that was increasingly fast moving, and was never interested in the tide of social change. In a changing world, Cézanne sought what might endure, painting above all the timeless and eternal. For him the few subjects from his region (*The Plaster Kiln*, also called the *Mill at the Trois-Sautets Bridge*), that had become more and more familiar over the years were sufficient: the area around the Jas de Bouffan, the woods of Château-Noir, the Bibémus Quarry... Cézanne was never a Gauguin, going off in search of "exotic" new themes, but rather with a bewildering stubbornness, he plugged away at his favorite themes. Among them was the theme of bathers. In fact, as this theme evolved, it is increasingly difficult to see it as involving bathing, strictly speaking. In the pictures treating this theme in the 1870's, water was still visible but thereafter it gradually disappeared as more and more attention was paid to the depicting of nude bodies and their relationship to the physical surroundings. The *Standing Female Nude* is an exceptional work for the normally prudish Cézanne by virtue of its size and its bold sensuality. Throughout his life, to conquer his fears and obsessions he strove to express his vision of the opposite sex in art. As he grew older and totally distant from Hortense, he nevertheless kept away from other women, apart from visits to the brothel. He sometimes spoke about these in his correspondence, a notable example being his letter to Zola of 25 August 1885: "All there is for me is total isolation from people. The brothel in town, or somewhere else, but nothing more. I pay up – nasty expression – but I need peace, and I get what I pay for... If only I had an indifferent family, everything would have been for the best." When he was living for most of the year in Aix, Cézanne gave up any idea of using female models, partly because of the prudishness of his family circle, but also because he never

Boy in a Red Waistcoat
1894/1895. Oil on canvas
80x65 cm
Zurich
Bührle Collection

managed to free himself totally from his fear and suspicion of women. Nevertheless, in a rather exceptional way in this watercolor, the artist studies female nudity with a detachment driven solely by a sense of creative enquiry. In this monumental work, woman is no longer the demonic seductress Olympia; on the other hand one cannot help recalling the *Temptations of Saint Anthony* painted some time previously by the artist surrounded by earthly delights and torments. Cézanne had aged in the interval and lost his perception of woman as a creature to be both admired and feared. Although it has sometimes been assumed so a little too quickly, it seems unlikely in fact that we are looking at Hortense in this picture, because by then, she no longer calmly agreed to pose for her husband. In his catalogue of the artist's work, Georges Rivière dates a nude in the Pellerin collection to 1898 (as it happens, the painting derived from this watercolor), and speaks of a certain "Marie-Louise, a model used on a few occasions by Cézanne". In fact, it is the only occasion, at least at the end of his career, when Cézanne is known to have painted a nude from life. This nude and the Vollard portrait were painted in the same studio that Cézanne occupied at various times in Montmartre, because the background in the two pictures is painted in identical colors. Yet, whereas Vollard was shown near the window, the nude was placed in front of a blank wall, and we know from Vollard himself, to whom the artist complained, that the latter was not satisfied with this model: "It's becoming very hard to work with female models! Yet I pay a lot for each session, it comes to around four francs, twenty sous more than before the war". The painting derived from the *Standing Female Nude* (now located in the United States) would have required countless hours and must have been based on the watercolor rather than painted directly from a life pose. The watercolor is probably also connected with Cézanne's preparations for his various *Large Bathers* (for example, the *Large Bathers* of 1898-1905). The first of these three compositions, on which Cézanne worked in Paris from 1895, contains a figure whose pose strongly resembles the model's. What the figures in these pictures are really doing is not clear, and their actions were progressively replaced by a repertory of elementary gestures. In the *Female Bathers* the figures are neatly arranged in two symmetrical groups in between which there is a central clear space, giving a perspective that lends depth to the picture. Since the third Impressionist exhibition, Cézanne's *Bathers* motif had been controversial. The

Portrait of Paul Cézanne in the countryside
Photo by Émile Bernard
1905. Proof on silver paper

Large Female Bathers
1898/1905. Oil on canvas
208x249 cm
Philadelphia
Philadelphia Museum of Art

Female Bathers
1883/1887. Pencil and watercolor
28x44 cm
Aix-en-Provence
Musée Granet

pictures were considered by admirers as being inspired by classical culture and dismissed out of hand by others as the work of an unskilled barbarian. The enthusiasts spoke of the naturalness and equilibrium of a classical composition and, paradoxically, it was the massive and hieratic appearance of Cézanne's figures (*Bathers*) that was regarded as a highly original feature. It has to be said that in these compositions, the female bathers somewhat resemble nymphs, and it was Rivière in 1877 who made the comparison with Antiquity, whereupon Cézanne turned it into a new pictorial theme. However one interprets this enigmatic series, the comparison does not really seem justified. The theme has been handled by a number of classic and modern artists (Titian, Rubens, Delacroix and Courbet, to name but a few) and is rather an invention of the Renaissance period. Cézanne was able to admire plenty of such works on his visits to the Louvre. A revealing detail says something about his inhibitions: the two sexes are strictly separated and never appear together on the same canvas. This contrasts with Renoir's practice at about this time, who depicted relaxed relations between males and females in groups (*Bathers*). Yet Cézanne shows men and women in the same theatrical poses and with the same range of suspended gestures (The *Bathers*, 1890-1900). Over the course of time, as the pictures supposedly imbued with classical inspiration gave way to the depiction of contemporary and anonymous bathers, we detect a freer handling of the subject. The anatomy of the bathers becomes even more unconventional. Cézanne boldly simplified his volumes (which had an impact on the next generation of painters), and his brushstrokes produced more and more geometrically delineated motifs, assimilating torsos and tree-trunks to the same figurative method. Cézanne was mainly concerned not about the individualization of the figures but the harmony produced by the interrelationship of landscape and figure. The three monumental *Large Bathers* (of which the Philadelphia version holds the record for the number of figures, seventeen!) were the culmination of his achievement in this theme. Merely taking into account the balanced composition of the picture, the Philadelphia *Bathers* is the most "classical" of the series, but it was unfinished despite the fact that Cézanne worked on it for seven years, from 1898 to 1905. On numerous parts of the canvas the clear ground (undercoat) can be seen, creating an effect of spontaneity and light, which is enhanced by the triangular gap breathing air into the middle of the

Bathers ●
1890/1892. Oil on canvas
60x82 cm
Paris
Musée d'Orsay

picture. The figures are a fundamental part of the structure of the work, and they echo the rhythms of the landscape. The standing nude on the left bends forward at exactly the same angle as the curving tree-trunk behind her. Matisse was fascinated by the masterly composition of this painting and incorporated this figure into his *Bathers* in 1909.

After 1890, while still working hard at developing his bather theme, Cézanne began a new series of paintings. These were portraits of country folk – peasants and farm girls – whose simplicity and solid, mute presence were just what he was looking for. As it happens, he felt a real human affinity with these sitters, representatives of a disappearing way of life to which he was greatly attached, and which was so different from the modernity he despised. These portraits, the last phase of his creative life, were for Cézanne a final opportunity to bring human beings back into a natural environment to which he could relate harmoniously, far from the world of passion and torment. For his *Cardplayers* he simply borrowed his models from among the tenant farmers of the Jas de Bouffan, setting up a studio in the farm for the purpose. Cézanne handled this subject at least five times, and always with the same sober setting and treatment. It was of course a classic, dating from France's great age, the seventeenth century, and Cézanne knew the *Cardplayers* of the school of Le Nain belonging to the Musée Granet in Aix. The large number of preliminary studies (*Study for the Cardplayers*) shows just how thoroughly he prepared the major finished versions. What we generally see is the players in frozen attitudes and, as here, much more often meditating about the game than putting down cards. In fact the human figures have no individuality and seem locked for all eternity in a motionless game of cards. The composition is firmly framed by particularly solid lines of axis, considerably reducing the importance of the surroundings. Unlike in classical painting, this treatment has no anecdotal or moralizing significance. Only the position of the bottle vis-à-vis the two players slightly decentralizes the axis of the picture, but the greater focusing on the player with the pipe is compensated by the color of the other player's jacket, a patch of light that fully brings him back into the picture despite the fact that his back is cut off at the edge of the canvas. The painting thus acquires a sort of meditative quality, and the same nobility is found in the celebrated *Woman with Coffee Pot*, painted not at the Jas de Bouffan but in Paris and depicting Cézanne's house cleaner. The

Bathers
1892/1894. Oil on canvas
24x25 cm
Paris
Musée d'Orsay

composition of this monumentally rigorous and symmetrical work is reinforced by the position of the spoon and the coffee pot. The tones are extremely delicate, especially in the paneling of the door, and accentuated by the exquisite motif of the flowers of the wallpaper, which are distant cousins of Monet's waterlilies, although given a more rigorous treatment by Cézanne. This picture brings out the solidity, not to say indestructibility, of the real world, and Cézanne confers timelessness to everyday activities and once again finds a way of relating the sitter to the surroundings. The last decades of Cézanne's life were, as we have seen, characterized by increasing horror of physical contacts even of the most trivial sort, and all his portraits reflect this neurotic concern for distance (*Madame Cézanne in the Greenhouse*). Ever since the time of their marriage, Hortense shared very little in her husband's life, and he is not known to have painted any portrait of her after about 1892. Here the sitter's face is deliberately blurred in order not to stand out too clearly against the general harmonious character of the composition. This splendid work demonstrates superb handling of color: an ochre background setting off the large blue expanse of the sitter's dress and the beautiful red of the flowers. In the same way, the cool tones of the shrub and the other vegetation contrast delicately with the warm background color. In the last part of his life, as in *The Smoker* except for the figures in his bathers series, Cézanne painted nothing but mature or elderly sitters, a choice which doubtless ties in with his hatred of artifice and the march of progress. *Young Man with Skull* inevitably reminding the viewer of Hamlet's meditation, points to a new religious consciousness in Cézanne as he reflects pessimistically upon existence. Its vanity increasingly preoccupied the embittered painter (*Self-Portrait at the Easel*). This pessimism can be detected in the melancholy poses of the figures and more obviously in the essentially classical theme of the death's head. But here too Cézanne, independently of the symbolic significance of the subject, reveals his fascination with the shape of the subject, simplifying and stylizing it geometrically. He owned several skulls, which can be found in other compositions used just like apples in a still life. If we ignore the meditative pose of the young man, the skull in this picture is treated in as familiar a way as the little table or a piece of cloth that are to be seen in so many other pictures. Another common Cézanne motif is the putto, or cupid, that we see in the *Still Life with Plaster Cupid*. He had great admiration for his fellow Provençal artist Pierre Puget, who was an architect and sculptor as well as a painter. Cézanne had always been impressed by the genius of this seventeenth-century artist, and had done a lot of pencil drawings of his work in the Louvre; he also had in his studio in the Lauves hills a plaster putto that was wrongly attributed to Puget. At all events, it is the one that we see in this still life. Like the blue cloth, it is found again in other paintings and numerous drawings. This attachment to a range of "fetichistic" accessories is one of the great constants of Cézanne's art. Vollard, for example, relates that

Bathers

1892/1894. Oil on canvas
22x33 cm
Paris
Musée d'Orsay

Cardplayers
1893/1896. Oil on canvas
47x57 cm
Paris
Musée d'Orsay

one morning the artist flew into a rage because "in a corner of the studio opposite to the one in which I was posing there was an old carpet on the floor that had been there for ever. It had lost its colors, and on that day, alas, the maid had taken it up with the admirable intention of beating it. Cézanne told me that it was unbearable not to see the carpet on the floor, and it would be impossible to continue with my portrait; indeed, he would never touch a paintbrush again in his life. He didn't keep his word, fortunately, but the fact remains that it was impossible for him to work again that day". In this picture the objects are carefully arranged around the putto, and on the floor to the right we see the bottom part of a painting after *The Flayed Man* attributed to Michelangelo and two other canvases. Cézanne's picture plays a sort of illusionist game: painted apples and real apples, the painting of a plaster cast and a real plaster cast, a painted tablecloth and a real one. The finish on this work is particularly thorough. We look down on the objects as if from a high vantage point. Although this type of perspective is to be found in a lot of his late work, it must be accounted for here partly by the restricted dimensions of the artist's studio, which did not allow him to move back far from his subject. In fact many of Cézanne's still lifes, which have this curious downward viewpoint, must have been painted in his studio in the Jas de Bouffan, where the limited space had consequences for the perspective. The plaster model, which is forty-six centimeters high, is painted larger than life, but the artist was not seeking to create an illusion of a three-dimensional world; rather he wished to depict another reality, that of the canvas, on a two-dimensional scale. As in other works of this period, he avoids the classic linear perspective that would have obliged him to paint every object in scale with everything else in the composition, whereas what he wanted above all was to allocate objects a size that seemed appropriate to him. From 1890, Cézanne placed more and more accessories into his still lifes and distributed them in dynamic equilibrium around the canvas, no longer in any way trying to capture a "real" scene. Henceforth, all that mattered was the interaction of form, matter and color, with the end product really being a landscape. A still life with a particularly full and complex content, Still Life with *Apples and Oranges* – first owned by Gustave Geffroy – is a supreme example of this. What we have here is a ravishing composition of apples, oranges and dishes arranged on a white cloth. Two different fabrics decorate the back-

Study for the cardplayers
1890/1892. Oil on canvas
50x46 cm
Paris
Musée d'Orsay

ground, a curtain with a foliage pattern and, on the left, a rug with a rectangular motif that was still to be seen in Cézanne's studio in Les Lauves on the eve of the Second World War. These materials and the tablecloth fill all the space around the still life objects, which relate to each other in an interplay of correspondences. Just as the full and round shape of the fruit bowl sets off the colorful fruit it contains, so the white ground of the canvas stands out visibly in the cloth at the bottom and to the left; and, as often in these still lifes, the folds of the cloth dramatically spill over the edge of the table. At the top and to the right, we should note the same dark brown wall,as in the Vollard portrait, which means that this picture was painted in 1898 or 1899 in Paris. The *Still Life with Onions* is another particularly sensitive work, composed of light and subtly varying shades, but set off against a large expanse of bare wall making up a plain background of unusual size by Cézanne's standards. Compared with *Apples and Oranges*, this picture is both more spacious and static. It is focused off-center, but the light folds of the cloth hanging over the table and the dark shape of the bottle create a compensatory sense of balance. The onion motif is also seen in the *Still Life with Plaster Cupid* of about the same date, but in that work the onions are marginal and less decorative. Here the forms of the fruit and onions are fully exploited decoratively in the foreground and the onion shoots have an arabesque quality.

In 1897, Cézanne's mother died, leaving him in considerable despondency. But it was also the year when one of his pictures was purchased by the National Gallery of Berlin. The year after, he worked at the Château-Noir location near Aix before setting off for Paris. In 1899, after a stay in Paris, he went back to Aix, where he was to spend the next five years virtually without interruption. This was the year when he suffered the painful experience of selling the Jas de Bouffan. Thereafter, while his wife and son lived mainly in Paris, he lived in a small flat in Aix with his housekeeper.

While *The Red Rock* was certainly painted in 1895, the other pictures of the Bibémus Quarry date mostly from 1897-1904. The Château-Noir site however had been painted by Cézanne as early as 1888. The Bibémus plateau is accessible via thorn-covered tracks up a cliffside and extends beyond the Château-Noir. Cézanne had been familiar with the wild beauty of these sites since his childhood, since this is where the Infernets Valley ended, at the other end of

Woman with Coffeepot
1890/1895. Oil on canvas
130x96 cm
Paris
Musée d'Orsay

**Madame Cézanne
in the Greenhouse**
1891/1892. Oil on canvas
92x73 cm
New York
Metropolitan Museum of Art

which Zola's father had built a dam to supply Aix with water. An unusual feature for a Cézanne composition is the brutal intrusion of the rock into the calm wooded landscape, which creates a starkly asymmetrical effect. This mass of mineral substance, by virtue of its color and treatment, forms a surprising contrast with the neatly hachured trees. The dramatic character of this landscape reflects Cézanne's passionate temperament in a very clear, not to say expressionist, way. By now he possessed the technique for bringing both serenity and strength to a sober recording of nature and at the same time expressing what he felt. The monochrome surface of the rock is deliberately intended to contrast with the intricate swirling brushstrokes and subtle blues and greens of the vegetation. Compared with the rigid diagonal pattern of earlier works, the vegetation here is handled more freely. A sense of balance is reestablished by the white marker stone on the bottom left in the middle of the vegetation. As with Bonnard, it is this seemingly insignificant detail that so often confers assurance on Cézanne's canvases. A picture painted roughly at the same period, *In the Château-Noir Park*), depicts the park surrounding a nineteenth-century building in the Viollet-le-Duc style; it is not far from the Bibémus Quarry and looks down on the road joining Tholonet and Aix. With its gothic arches and bulk, Château-Noir was at that time a strange architectural intrusion amid the classical landscape surrounding the village. The wild beauty of the site captivated Cézanne and he tried to acquire the property after selling the Jas de Bouffan. The building was a curious neo-gothic venture made up of two unfinished wings linked by an orangerie that was also unfinished. Cézanne's friend Gasquet, a writer from Aix, described it thus:"...the Château-Noir, which is also called the Devil's Castle, is the fantasy of a coal and soot merchant whose business had prospered. He had it built and then painted black from top to bottom. Fortunately sun and rain in time lightened the façade. It was a golden color with a red tiled roof, set between clumps of green pines, when Cézanne lived there, such as we so often see it in the last great landscapes that he painted in this region." There were numerous subjects here for Cézanne, and he painted a great number of watercolors as well as oils of the same subject. Of the château itself, Cézanne at first was drawn only to the surroundings, because from within the grounds there was a view of Mont Sainte-Victoire in all its majesty. He would set up his easel in the shade of the trees near the Château (the unspoilt environment of trees and rocks was a favorite theme), then between 1895 and 1898 his easel moved closer to the main subject, the strange property itself (*Château-Noir*). Around 1900 Cézanne was sometimes accompanied by a group of painter friends led by Joseph Ravaisou, a fervent local champion of his work. *The view of Château-Noir*, painted in 1905, perfectly exemplifies his conception of art with regards to nature in his last years, that of a totally independent and objective artist transcending realism to attain detachment and freedom. His brushstrokes are slanting in the sky and vertical in the rest of the canvas and applied generously and with masterful assurance, but despite this different alignment of the brushstrokes the sky and trees almost merge: Cézanne was in the process of achieving perfect unity in his art. André Malraux referred to the astonishingly muted colors of this work when remarking upon the colors of a thirteenth-century painted scroll kept in Kyoto: "...In the west, matt immediately suggests fresco. But there is shade in fresco... I have only ever found the contents of this scroll in the Château-Noir in the Picasso collection: Vollard, faithful to Cézanne's wishes, did not varnish it."

Once the Jas de Bouffan was sold, Cézanne had only a small studio in Aix to work in and rooms he rented in the outbuildings of the Château. To the bitter disappointment of the artist, the owner would not sell the property itself. So in 1902, Cézanne had a large studio built to his own design on the road at Lauves (to the north and slightly above Aix), and slowly gave up painting at Château-Noir and Bibémus. Rivière left us with an extremely lively description of this new studio: "The rustic house at Lauves was of the greatest simplicity and even then it was not as simple as the artist would have like it to be. On the side where the road was, it was protected by a high wall and you could hardly see it from the outside. The olivetrees and a few other trees hid it from the gaze of the immediate neighbors. The studio was a large square room with an appropriately high ceiling. The furniture was minimal: two easels streaked with paint, a few rustic chairs, a sort of divan resembling a camp bed, a small kitchen table

The Smoker
c. 1895. Oil on canvas
92x73 cm
St Petersburg
Ermitage Museum

Self-portrait

1898/1900. Pencil
33x26 cm
Aix-en-Provence
Musée Granet

and another long and low one, both in pine and covered in dust and stains. That was all." Whereas Cézanne had known the Jas de Bouffan even before becoming a painter, the Lauves studio became the one place in Aix exclusively dedicated to his needs. There he untiringly devoted himself to depicting his old friend, the Sainte-Victoire, a subject that can be considered for Cézanne as an invocation of the immutable and eternal forces of nature. Around the period 1898-1900, even before the Lauves studio was built, he painted it once more (*La Montagne Sainte-Victoire seen from Bibémus*). After painting it so many times, he could still discover fresh harmonies (*Montagne Sainte-Victoire from Les Lauves*). Cézanne's palette is restricted here to just four colors, violet, ochre, blue and green, but he coordinates and sets them off masterfully in a particularly dynamic way. Over the whole surface of the canvas, the light and dark tones alternate in an austere rhythmic pattern and the three foreground tones have a remarkably powerful impact. The elements of the landscape are united by the nuances within the range of tones used and by the parallel-line brushwork. The National Gallery of Scotland's *Montagne Sainte Victoire* was painted at the same time as the previous work and is of high plastic definition. It is perhaps Cézanne's last picture of his beloved mountain, but the exact place where he set up his easel is unknown, nor is it known whether it was painted in autumn or spring. The very delicate range of tones suggests it must have been one or the other of these seasons and the sharply delineated branches in the foreground, contrasting forcefully with the soft lines of the background, are bare of leaves. This shows at any rate just how normally unrelated Cézanne's work was at this time to anything specific or ephemeral: there is not only no perceptible human trace but no detail indicating the seasons. We could not be further away from the series of pictures painted by Monet, for example, who was concerned to record the passage of time and the differences of color and light dur-

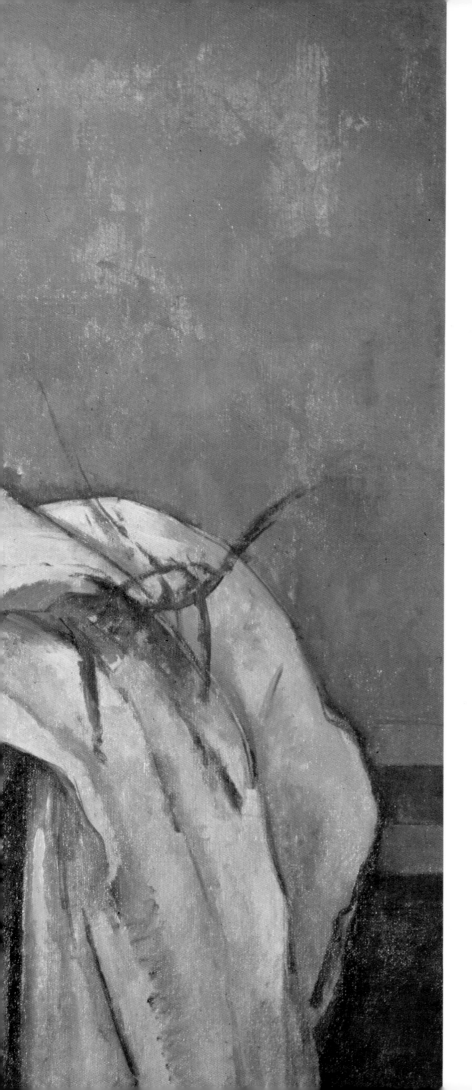

Still life with Onions
c. 1895. Oil on canvas
66x82 cm
Paris
Musée d'Orsay

Young Man with Skull
1894/1896. Oil on canvas
130x97 cm
Merion
Barnes Fundation

ing the annual cycles of nature. The scene was perhaps painted in the morning, as the colors seem to suggest that the sun is not yet bringing much light into the landscape. The brushwork shows evidence of much panache and enthusiasm, but the canvas is not completely covered.

While Cézanne was quietly continuing with his painting in the open air, a change of perception was slowly taking place with regards to the status of his work, and the increase in the number of exhibitions says something about the interest that critics and the public were taking in it. In 1899, he held a new solo exhibition at Vollard's gallery, and this time his canvases fetched considerable sums. The following year, Cassirer organized a similar exhibition in Berlin, but this time without a single sale being made. In 1903, the year of Pissarro's death and one year after Zola's, the latter's collection of art was put up for sale, and his Cézannes went for an average price of 1 500 francs, a healthy sum. That same year, Cézanne had work on show at the Vienna Secession. In 1904, he had a visit from Émile Bernard who watched him at work. He also exhibited in the Paris Autumn Show (Salon d'automne), and in the Berlin gallery of Cassirer for the second time. All this public attention and commercial activity nevertheless in no way interrupted the artist's unchanging rhythm of life, and he kept on painting in his beloved region of Aix, as we see in *Winding Road near Aix* and in the contemporary *Aix Cathedral*. This latter work, a fine piece, was painted from the window of the Lauves studio. We know what Cézanne thought about progress and its consequences and he said to Émile Bernard one day that "the Highways Department had disfigured Aix and we had better be quick if we still wanted to see something before it all goes". During these last years Cézanne used watercolor more and more for his studies, and one can discern a clear interaction between the characteristics of this medium and his work in oil. This can be seen in his watercolor *La Montagne Sainte-Victoire* where the swiftly executed brushstrokes do not follow the lines of the preliminary sketch and the subjects seen from a distance form themselves on their own in the light.

Cézanne's Studio in Aix-en-Provence
Viollet Collection

Still life
with Plaster Cupid
1895. Oil on paper laid on wood
71x57 cm
London
Courtauld Institute

Château-Noir
1900/1904. Oil on canvas
73x96 cm
Washington
National Gallery of Art

● **In the Château-Noir Park**
1900. Oil on canvas
92x73 cm
Paris
Musée de l'Orangerie

Château-Noir
1904/1906. Oil on canvas
74x94 cm
Paris
Musée Picasso

**The Tholonet Road
and Montagne Sainte-Victoire in 1900**
Aix-en-Provence

**La Montagne Sainte-Victoire
seen from the Bibémus Quarry**
1897. Oil on canvas
65x81 cm
Baltimore
Museum of Art

**La Montagne Sainte-Victoire
seen from Les Lauves**
1902/1904. Oil on canvas
69x89 cm
Philadelphia
Philadelphia Museum of Art

La Montagne Sainte-Victoire
1900/1902. Gouache, pencil
and watercolor
31x47 cm
Paris
Louvre, D.A.G. (fonds Orsay)

Aix Cathedral
1900/1906. Pencil and
watercolor
32x48 cm
Paris
Musée Picasso

Apples and Oranges
1895/1900. Oil on canvas
74x93 cm
Paris
Musée d'Orsay

Kitchen table
jugs and bottles
1902/1906. Pencil and watercolor
21x27 cm
Paris
Louvre, D.A.G. (fonds Orsay)

Still life

Apples, Pears and Pans

1900/1904. Watercolor and pencil

28x47 cm

Paris

Louvre, D.A.G. (fonds Orsay)

**Gray Earthware Jug
owned by Paul Cézanne**
Paris
Musée d'Orsay

**Still life with Fruit,
Carafe, Sugarbowl and Bottle**
1900/1906. Watercolor on pencil
31x43 cm
Paris
Louvre, D.A.G. (fonds Orsay)

The economy of means deployed in this fine watercolor reminds us of what we noted in *The Montagne Sainte-Victoire with the Tall Pinetree*: thinly applied, restricted color, with the brushstrokes juxtaposed or overlapping and allowing the whiteness of the canvas to cause the dabs of paint to shimmer. At the same time, Cézanne was also doing more still lifes in watercolor (*Kitchen Table: Jugs and Bottles*) and this latest genre, just like his portraits, displays the perfect balance of a masterly composition at the same time as a feeling of sensuality and happiness. On the death of Cézanne, most of his work was still shunned, but his watercolors were admired not just by the public but also by the cream of the next generation of painters. It was the watercolors that caused Cézanne's talent to be generally recognized, just as, like the landscapes, they brought discipline to his sense of composition and the perfection of his technique. In *Still Life with Apples, Pears and Saucepan* an extraordinarily luminous watercolor, we see once again the theme of fruit. This was a favorite with Cézanne partly because it was inherently neutral emotionally and he could give expression to his own sensations, and also because he could arrange the fruit as he liked while still doing life painting. Whereas dabs of especially bright primary colors give volume to the fruit with a remarkably graceful and flowing touch, the outlines of the accessories are edged in blue. More applications of primary colors lead the eye to focus on the foreground, the handle of the saucepan sticking out where the colors converge. Gasquet left an interesting account of the way time passed when Cézanne was working in his Lauves studio: "He worked at whatever it was he was painting, a portrait, landscape, still life, either in the studio or out in the fields. In between the sessions, which lasted an hour or hour and a quarter, he spent five minutes leafing through some book: two or three pages of Sainte-Beuve or Charles Blanc, the very dusty, venerable treatise on anatomy by Tortebat - a member of the Academy of the Beaux-Arts, he liked to stress - dating from the seventeenth century. His volume of Baudelaire's poetry, dropping to pieces, with its binding falling apart, was always somewhere close to hand. On the walls, there was a big engraving in a black frame, Delacroix's *Sardanapalus*, a photograph fixed with four drawing pins of the *Sirens* by Rubens, and the *Romans of the Decadence* by Couture, a highly thought of academic painter who used his influence to prevent any nonconformist painters getting into the Salon. In a red velvet case on the ground, or on the little paintbrush table, or on a chair, but always locked, was the small, elaborately framed canvas of Delacroix's *Hagar in the Desert*, which he had copied. For a month he also pinned David's *Sabines* to the wall, referring to it with an ironic sigh, and sometimes Daumier and Forain drawings cut out from newspapers."

Maurice Denis
The Visit to Paul Cézanne
1906. Watercolor and pencil
25x31 cm
Paris
Musée d'Orsay

Maurice Denis
Homage to Cézanne
1900/1904. Oil on canvas
180x240 cm
Paris
Musée d'Orsay

Towards the end of his life he stopped painting Hortense and his son altogether, and it was at this stage that he found in his gardener Vallier (*The Gardener*) a model who was always available and one of the last people whom he felt he could trust, together with his old housekeeper, Mme Brémond. He painted Vallier some ten times in oil or watercolor, always sitting out of doors. In this full length painting, left uncompleted, the model is sitting on a stool on the studio terrace in light dappled by foliage. The yellow painted wall of the studio can be seen to the left, and to the right the dark greens of the vegetation in the garden. Sitters often posed with folded arms in the late portraits, and as well as perhaps reflecting the artist's own introversion, the pose is a more patent reminder of the melancholy images of saints that Cézanne could have admired countless times in the Aix-en-Provence museum. The perfect harmony between sitter and natural setting is the culmination of Cézanne's lifelong artistic quest. It was thus in portraits of humble individuals rather than in his innumerable bathers that he achieved his dream of total unity between sitter and nature.

The summer of 1906 was particularly scorching, and although the aging painter was much fatigued by the heat, he nevertheless frequently went out to his favorite spots to paint in watercolor. On 15 October, he was caught in a heavy rainstorm while painting out of doors and had to wait a long time in the rain before being brought home in a passing cart. This took a lot out of him and he had to take to his bed two days later. A malicious rumor of the time has it that Hortense kept an appointment with her dressmaker rather than take the first train to Aix on hearing that her husband was on his deathbed. At all events, she and her son arrived too late: the great artist had died of pneumonia on the morning of 22 October. The last word goes to one of Cézanne's few contemporaries lucky enough to see him in a late burst of creative activity. Shortly after his death, his friend and fellow Aix painter, Joseph Ravaisou, published a fine article about the great man: "Cézanne is perhaps the most exact and the most realistic of painters of our time... He works by very simple observations. For example, instead of deconstituting the elements of the light values that give depth and blueness to skies, without any analysis, he just makes what he calls a sensation of blue, and this sensation is as fresh and strong as ever on the tip of his brush. He captures the immaterial character of the atmosphere, going far further than any open-air painter into the art of expressing abstractions. Yet these abstractions are inherent in the nature of the objects depicted, and all that is meant by nature is nothing other than the quantity of truth perceived in these objects by the artist's eye. So between abstraction and realism there is only an apparent contradiction; it is even impossible for a painting to be true if it is intended only to imitate the model. To copy nature is folly; one copies neither air, nor movement, nor light, nor life. That was Cézanne's opinion. His portraits, landscapes, still lifes and nude studies all confirm as much the durability of his manner as the steadfastness of his sincerity. He was a voluptuary in art. He was passionate in his love of Nature, perhaps exclusively so; he painted to prolong his joy of living among the trees... In this pious exile, he exalted his faith to the level of a miracle: the mystery of the blue beyond was revealed to him." If "no man is prophet in his own country", there is no greater proof of it than Cézanne; we can be quite certain that the master painter would have appreciated this homage from a fellow citizen of Aix.

The Gardener
1900/1906. Oil on canvas
63x52 cm
London
Tate Gallery

Boat and Bathers

1888/1891. Pencil and watercolor
30x125 cm
Paris
Musée de l'Orangerie

...trait de Cézanne peignan...
Aix en Provence
Janvier 1904.

CONCLUSION

Cézanne's misanthropy was not totally unjustified, since he was proved right in the end. Without his unswerving determination to pursue his aims despite doubt and discouragement, the horde of uncomprehending detractors might have got the better of the master of modern art. Painting was the only life's joy and the only passion of Cézanne, and it has to be admitted that art was all he lived for, everything else being of minor importance. Throughout his life, with his eye as penetrating as his mind, he sought tirelessly to comprehend the perceptible world around him with the gaze that every painter must have, that of the visionary, yet his progression was not effortless. The first marker on the long road towards reemphasizing the structure of things and bringing back a solid pictorial framework into the art of his time was put down about 1870. This was when he moved from his "exotic" period with his violent impasto effects to a more linear style. But although impressionism was just a phase for Cézanne, he was shrewd enough to realize that its techniques were taking him in the right direction and could help him conquer his unstable temperament. Impressionism did indeed help Cézanne to discipline his themes, but the pictures painted after 1870 are different from his youthful work above all because of their light palette and new sense of composition, and this was a vital stage in his evolution. It was also at this time that Cézanne developed the distinctive brushstroke that became his classic manner

Paul Cézanne in Provence
c. 1890.

from 1880 onwards: the light touches with the tip of the brush learnt from Pissarro turned gradually into parallel, juxtaposed strokes covering the whole of the canvas. They were applied energetically and their systematic alignment was an important factor in the shaping of the subject. Yet there was still a major gulf between Cézanne and the Impressionists: their art recorded the ephemeral, whereas he desired above all to paint what was immutable in nature. Contrary to their quest for the fleeting moment and the shimmering effect of light on surfaces, he was attracted to what was permanent. Similarly, creating an idyllic atmosphere and dissolving the material substance of the world in a pool of light was the polar opposite of the art that Cézanne wished to invent, an art far from some sensitive contemplative state. Thus at the beginning of the 1880s, while he was establishing the range of his themes (still life with fruit, bathing scene, portrait, landscape) and eschewing traditional techniques for creating depth, Cézanne abandoned all concern for anecdotal and atmospheric incidentals; transience gave way to stability and duration. Cézanne's mature style was one of fusion, born of the wish to link form to color and bring together all the elements of reality in a strong, all-encompassing unity. Henceforth time was built in to the structure of the composition pictorially, crystallizing all the changes of nature in a new order, somewhat resembling a new geological organization. Thanks to logical and well thought out composition, Cézanne sought via the color system of his canvases to capture the enduring appearance of the world. He conceived the subject as a conscious uniting of matter and color. He was in fact the first to organize the deceptive illusion of appearances by reducing this illusion to a geometrical structure, but was at the same time skillful enough to avoid the effect of aridity that might have resulted. His sensibility prevented him from succumbing to the temptation of making it mechanical. Using strict discipline, Cézanne endeavored to "reconstruct" nature on the canvas according to his own conceptions, and, far from obscuring the subject, this process brought it out in all the reality of its structure: Cézanne painted the world the way one peels an orange, to discover the treasure concealed within. The treasure was twofold: first, seeing the truth of the subject stripped of outdated illusionist artifice (trying to recreate a three-dimensional world on a two-dimensional surface); secondly and above all, discovering the way ahead for painting at a time when photography was increasingly being considered the medium for reproducing the tangible world, and no progress seemed possible in painting since the time of the Impressionists. The age was in fact propitious; the art of a new era accepted the challenge, and the first wave was led by the leaders of the cubist revolution. Cézanne could rest in peace. For the centuries ahead his canvases were to enrich the greatest museums of the world. The master of Aix had triumphed over rejection by the Salon and denigration by the critics...

BIBLIOGRAPHY

John Rewald,	*Cézanne, Geffroy et Gasquet*, followed by *Souvenirs sur Cézanne* by Louis Aurenche and *Lettres inédites*, Paris, Les Quatre-Chemins, 1959
Marianne Bourges	*Les Itinéraires de Cézanne*, fascicle published by the city of Aix-en-Provence, 1984
Denis Coutagne	*Cézanne, avant-après*, Éditions Critérion, Paris, 1989
Raymond Jean	*Cézanne, la Vie, l'Espace*, Éditions du Seuil, Paris, 1986
Raymond Jean	*Quand Cézanne et Zola se rencontrent*, Éditions Actes Sud, Arles, 1992
Léo Larguier	*Le Dimanche avec Paul Cézanne*, L'Édition, 1926
Gilles Plazy	*Le Goût de la Provence de Paul Cézanne*, Éditions du Chêne, Paris, 1995
John Rewald	*Cézanne et Zola*, Éditions A. Sedrowski, Paris, 1936
John Rewald	*Paul Cézanne*, correspondence with notes and preface by John Rewald, Grasset, Paris, 1972
John Rewald	*Les Aquarelles de Cézanne*, descriptive catalogue, Flammarion, Paris, 1984
John Rewald,	*Cézanne, une biographie*, Flammarion, A.M.G., Paris, 1990
Georges Rivière	*Le Maître Paul Cézanne*, Floury Éditeur, Paris, 1923
Ambroise Vollard	*Cézanne*, Éditions Grès et Cie, Paris, 1914
Frank Elgar	*Cézanne*, Somogy, Paris, 1968
Mario de Micheli	*Cézanne*, Flammarion, Paris, 1968
Ambroise Vollard	*En écoutant Cézanne, Degas, Renoir*, Éditions Grasset, Paris, 1938
Émile Zola	*L'Œuvre*, Paris, 1886
Marianne Bourges	*Cézanne en son atelier*, fascicle published by the city of Aix-en-Provence, 1982
Louis Aurenche	*Souvenirs de ma jeunesse sur Paul Cézanne*, Les Quatre-Chemins, Paris, 1960
John Rewald	*Choquet et Cézanne*, Gazette des Beaux-Arts, juillet-août 1969, pp. 33-96
Richard W. Murphy	*Cézanne et son temps*, Time Life, 1971
Denis Coutagne	*Cézanne en Provence*, Éditions Assouline, Paris, 1995
Marcel Brion	*Cézanne*, Fabbri, Milan, 1972
P.-M. Doran	*Conversations avec Cézanne*, critical edition, Éditions Macula, Paris, 1978
Michel Hoog	*L'Univers de Cézanne*, Scrépel, Paris, 1971
Joachim Gasquet	*Cézanne*, Éditions Berhneim-Jeune, Paris, 1926
Peter Handke	*La Leçon de la Sainte-Victoire*, Éditions Gallimard, Paris, 1981
Michel Hoog	*Cézanne puissant et solitaire*, Découvertes Gallimard - Réunion des musées nationaux, Paris, 1989

PHOTOGRAPHIC CREDITS

AKG Paris : p. 10, 30/31, 65, 72, 117, 118/119, 145, 148/149, 164, 167, 172, 176/177, 190, 196

AKG Paris/Erich Lessing : cover, p. 2, 5, 6, 8, 17, 20, 25, 26, 28, 40/41, 44, 46/47, 54, 57, 59, 60/61, 64, 68, 74, 78, 84, 86/87, 88, 91, 94, 97, 101, 114/115, 128/129, 132/133, 134, 141, 153, 158/159, 163, 170/171, 175, 178, 183, 188/189, 207

AKG Paris/Erich Lessing © Adagp, Paris 2002 : p.194/195

Artephot : p. 58, 112, 181

Collection Sirot-Angel : p. 200

Henry Ely, Aix-en-Provence : p. 80, 130,180, 182

L'Illustration/Keystone : p. 202

Musée Granet, Aix-en-Provence : p. 56, 168

Philadelphia Museum of Art : p. 184/185

RMN : p. 24, 36g, 66, 69, 83, 102/103, 109, 123, 150/151, 155, 193

RMN/Arnaudet : p. 14, 29, 32, 48, 49, 70, 71, 99, 107, 197/198

RMN/Bellot : p. 36d, 38g, 63, 76/77, 136, 191, 192

RMN/Berizzi : p. 38d, 85, 113, 126, 127, 131, 143, 186, 187

RMN/Berizzi © Adagp, Paris 2002 : p. 195

RMN/Blot : p. 19, 22, 37, 42, 43, 62, 82, 104, 105, 121

RMN/Lewandowski : p. 34, 53, 55, 67, 81, 116, 124/125, 138, 156, 160

RMN/Ojeda : p. 110, 179, 205

RMN/Ojeda © Adagp, Paris 2002 : p. 13, 146

Roger-Viollet : p. 174

The Art Institute of Chicago : p. 92/93

Printed and bound in China